T FALSIFICATION OF AFRIKAN CONSCIOUSNESS

Eurocentric History, Psychiatry and the Politics of White Supremacy

Amos N. Wilson

THE
FALSIFICATION
OF
AFRIKAN
CONSCIOUSNESS

*Eurocentric History, Psychiatry
and the Politics of White Supremacy*

Amos N. Wilson

New York 1993
Afrikan World InfoSystems
Afrikanworld@aol.com

FIFTH PRINTING December 2002

Producer and Editor: SABABU N. PLATA

Assistant Editor: Adisa Makalani

Cover design: Joseph Gillians

ISBN: 1-879164-02-7 (soft cover)
ISBN: 1-879164-11-6 (case bound)

Library of Congress Catalog Control No. 98-164518

AFRIKAN WORLD INFOSYSTEMS
743 Rogers Avenue Suite 6
Brooklyn, New York 11226
E-mail: Afrikanworld@aol.com

Printed in the USA

Dedication

To: Sababu N. Plata
Joe Gillians

True incarnations of brotherly love

Other Books by Amos N. Wilson

About the Author

Professor AMOS N. WILSON is a former social case worker, supervising probation officer, psychological counselor, training administrator in the New York City Department of Juvenile Justice, and Assistant Professor of Psychology at the City University of New York.

Born in Hattiesburg, Mississippi in 1941, Amos completed his undergraduate degree at the acclaimed Morehouse College in Atlanta, Georgia. He later migrated to New York where he attained his Ph.D. from Fordham University in New York City.

Familiarly referred to as Brother Amos, he availed himself for numerous appearances at educational, cultural and political organizations such as the First World Alliance, the Afrikan Poetry Theatre, Afrikan Echoes, House of Our Lord Church, the Patrice Lumumba Coalition, the Slave Theatre, and CEMOTAP to name just a few. His travels took him throughout the United States, to Canada and the Caribbean.

Dr. Wilson's activities transcended academia into the field of business, owning and operating various enterprises in the greater New York area.

CONTENTS

Part I

European Historiography and Oppression Exposed
An Afrikan Analysis and Perspective

Part II

Eurocentric Political Dogmatism
Its Relationship to the Mental Health Diagnosis of Afrikan People

Contents

Part III

The Political Psychology
of Black Consciousness

Editor's Note:

The lecture *European Historiography and Oppression Exposed: An Afrikan Analysis and Perspective*, is part of a presentation by the author at Afrikan Echoes, a community-based (still flourishing) cultural institution located in Newark, New Jersey, on February 5, 1989. The second lecture, *Eurocentric Political Dogmatism: Its Relationship to the Mental Health Diagnosis of Afrikan People*, a sterling critique of the criminal justice and mental health establishments, was delivered at Harlem Hospital on January 15, 1985.

From time to time, attendees at the aforementioned lectures and others within their resonances have asked whether they are available in print. Ably assisted by Adisa Makalani and Ralph King, these requests have been honored whereby these trenchant lectures have now been transcribed, edited, indexed, and readied for dissemination.

Furthermore, in keeping pace with technological and communications advancements and enthusiastic enquiring, we have made available on audio tape and compact disk an extensive list of Professor Wilson's presentations. In addition we have made this publication, *TheFalsification of Afrikan Consciousness,* and the heavyweight *Blueprint For Black Power*, available in limited edition library bound impressive hard cover. Our next Wilson publication is well afoot under the working title *The Psychology of Self-Hatred and Self-Defeat.* This we expect will be released in early 2003. Please look to our web page (presently under construction) for products, audio clips, new innovations and breaking news on our endeavors.

In closing, we at Afrikan World InfoSystems feel esteemed by your requests, inquiries and patronage, not to mention letters of suggestion and commendation — especially from students and our kin locked away within walls of incarceration. Humbled, yet encouraged, we forge ahead, inducting, ever expanding the domain of discourse, providing insight and foresight to those seeking enlightenment and liberation. *Asante Sana.*

—*Sababu N. Plata*
December, 2002

Introduction

THE PSYCHOLOGY, CONSCIOUSNESS and behavioral tendencies of individuals and societies are to a very significant extent the products of their personal and collective histories. Both personal and collective psychology are constructed from those experiences which can be consciously retrieved from memory as well as those experiences which have been forgotten or repressed but which still represent themselves in individual and collective habits, tendencies, traditions, emotional responsivities, perspectives, ways of processing information, attitudes and reflex-like reactions to certain stimuli and situations. Both types of experiences interacting with current perceptions are utilized by individuals and groups to achieve certain material and non-material ends.

The psychology of individuals and groups may also, in part, be constructed from "historical and experiential amnesia". That is, when an individual or a group is compelled by various circumstances to repress important segments of his or its formative history he or it at the same time loses access to crucially important social, intellectual and technical skills associated with that history which could be used to resolve current problems. Consequently, to some lesser or greater degree, the individual or group may be handicapped or disadvantaged by the resulting amnesia. Finally, individual and group psychology are in part constructed from the perception he or it has of his or its history, the inferences drawn from that history about the kind of person or group he or it may be, what other persons or groups think of him or it, and the destiny that awaits him or it.

The character of individual and collective consciousness and the range of their behavioral possibilities and very significantly

1

influenced by the quality of their recordings and recollections of their historical experiences. To manipulate history is to manipulate consciousness; to manipulate consciousness is to manipulate possibilities; and to manipulate possibilities is to manipulate power.

Herein lies the mortal threat of Eurocentric historiography to Afrikan existence. For what must be the form and functionality of Afrikan consciousness and behavior if they are derivative of an Afrikan history written by their oppressors? The history of the oppressed, as written by their oppressors, shape the consciousness and psychology of both oppressed and oppressor. It helps to legitimate the oppressive system and to maintain the imbalance of power in favor of the oppressor. Eurocentric history writing is essentially an exercise in publishing apologetics for the European oppression of Afrikan peoples; often a gross and crude attempt to create and shape a subordinate and inferior Afrikan consciousness and psychology. It seeks to impose a social/historical/cultural amnesic tax on the heads of Afrikan peoples and thereby rob them of their most valuable resources — their knowledge of truth and reality of self; their cultural heritage and identity, minds, bodies, and souls; their wealth, lands, products of their labor and lives.

Eurocentric historiography is the most formidable ally of White racism and imperialism. Its treacherous role in this regard must be explored and reversed by an Afrikan-centered historiography written by Afrikan historians dedicated to historical accuracy and truth — historians who are unafraid to speak truth to power.

The clarion call for the writing of a restorative Afrikan-centered historiography — a critical undertaking — is a call for the healing of the wounds of Afrikan peoples; for Afrikan unity; for the freeing and expansion of Afrikan consciousness; for the reconquest of Afrikan minds, bodies, lands, resources, and Afrikan autonomy.

Every Eurocentric social institution conspires with Eurocentric historiography to handcuff and incarcerate Afrikan consciousness, to justify and facilitate the subordination and exploitation of Afrikan peoples.

One such institution is the Eurocentric mental health establishment.

A product and functionary of European imperialism this establishment promulgates explanatory systems, diagnostic techniques, labeling and treatment regimes which obscure the true origins of Afrikan mental *dis*eases and maladaptiveness — the effects and aftereffects of White supremacy. By these means this establishment makes its most important contribution, along with Eurocentric historiography, to the falsification and misdirection of Afrikan consciousness and behavior.

In the context of a racist social system, psychological diagnosis, labeling and treatment of the behavior of politically oppressed persons are political acts performed to attain political ends. For oppression begins as a psychological fact and is in good part a psychological state. If oppression is to operate with maximum efficiency, it must become and remain a psychological condition achieving self-perpetuating motion by its own internal dynamics and by its own inertial momentum.

The Eurocentric mental health establishment, a beneficiary of the White domination of Afrikan peoples, is a very important cog in this self-perpetuating machine. Its reason for being is to nurture and sanction the imperialist and racist regime which fathered it. Thus its explanatory systems and its treatment approaches ultimately must be exposed as political ideology and oppressive political governance parading as empirically validated principles of psychological and medical science, and as "objective" psychotherapeutic and psychiatric practices. The Eurocentric mental health establishment consequently cannot provide adequate explanations, rationales, preventative and remedial practices for Afrikan peoples whose psychology is derivative of a singularly unique history and cultural experience and of a necessarily revolutionary drive to achieve liberation from subordination.

Eurocentric historiography — the biasing and falsification of history in ways which justify White supremacy — is not merely the fiddle-faddle of absent-minded professors ensconced in academic ivory towers. It involves a deliberate and serious exercise in myth-making, in the development of Eurocentric cultural mythic thought which rationalizes a concrete social order founded on the perpetual subordination of Afrikan peoples to European peoples. Moreover, the Eurocentric social order, which the European historiographic and behavioral science establishments legitimate and support, is essentially a "social machine" which manufactures a consciousness and behavioral orientation in Afrikan peoples designed to serve the purposes of White supremacy. In this volume we begin an exploration of the working mechanisms of the machine and the means by which it is to be dismantled.

The healing of the collective Afrikan body, mind and spirit, the expansion of Afrikan consciousness, calls for the accelerated advancement of Afrikan-centered historiographic, social and natural sciences, the development of incisive critical disciplines which can make decisive contributions to the establishment of a new world social order in which all humanity are free of oppression and degradation.

It is our hope that the two lectures and the appended essay included herein will make positive contributions to this end.

Amos N. Wilson

Part One

EUROPEAN HISTORIOGRAPHY AND OPPRESSION EXPOSED

An Afrikan Analysis and Perspective

I

AFTER LERONE BENNETT, JR. in his book, *Black Power U.S.A.*, reviewed [Black political] history and presented it so magnificently, I looked for the summary chapter which would tell us that what we had during Reconstruction was not *real* power. In fact, the name of the book is a misnomer. I was looking for him to say that the rights and the freedom of a people are not protected by law only. That, to me, seemed to be the lesson that was taught there: laws in and of themselves will not protect us; laws are words written on paper; laws protect no one.

Laws are no stronger than those who enforce them. President Rutherford B. Hayes taught us that lesson quite clearly. The day that the federal government decided not to enforce the Reconstruction laws, the so-called freedom of Black people came to an end. Laws were on the books, but who cared? The Supreme Court reneged in the 1870s and we were almost back where we started.

The Supreme Court can and does change its mind. It can rule one way at one point and reverse its ruling at another. Where does that leave us? We see it happening to us all the time. Ultimately, it means that we can only protect our rights and interests as people, not through laws written by other people and laws enforced by other people, but through the power to prevent other people from having their way with us. The emphasis, then, should be on the development of *true* power: military, economic and otherwise. That is our ultimate salvation.

If it arises at some point in the future that Whites have to make a decision between feeding their children and ours, irrespective of what kind of laws are on the books they are going to feed theirs and starve ours. We can apply to the Supreme

Court and anywhere else we choose, nevertheless, the situation will be exactly the way they wish it to be. Therefore, relying on laws — *new* Reconstruction laws — and promises almost exclusively are a very poor sort of salvation and assurance for our survival as a people. There is no way around it. We have to attain true and real power. This should be our goal. Allow me to indulge in a brief review of the first Reconstruction 1867-1877.

Progression and Regression in Reconstruction History[a]

Many of us in Black Studies who are reconstructing history (the history of the United States) think that we are entering a new era in American history. We may think that the things we are witnessing today, i.e., the election of Blacks to political office and their appointments to various positions, their accomplishments in various corporations and so forth, are something new in American history. Yet the study of Reconstruction history should quickly convince us that we are currently undergoing *deja vu.*

Many of us view history as a continuing progression upward and onward. We have bought the American concept of progress: the idea that things must over time necessarily get better. There is no law in the universe that tells us our future survival is assured; that we will continue to exist now and into the future. There have been races and ethnic groups who have been virtually wiped out on this planet. There is no guarantee that our own group will not be wiped out as well. The idea that we must necessarily arrive at a point greater than that reached by our ancestors could possibly be an illusion. The idea that somehow according to some great universal principle we are going to be in a better condition than our ancestors is an illusion which often results from *not* studying history and recognizing that progressions and regressions occur; that integrations and disintegrations occur in history.

History is not a fairy tale wherein certain things are accomplished and people live happily ever after. Many of us think the accomplishments we have made up to this point mean that we are only going to expand them in the future. We had better think about that again. I will point out today why we must not be so optimistic as to be foolish.

Let us go back for a moment to an article written in *Ebony* magazine, October 1981, wherein Lerone Bennett wrote (I think) his conclusion to his book *Black Power U.S.A.* When I finished reading that book, I felt that the last chapter was missing. It went on to laud Black Power during the Reconstruction era and so forth and yet, somehow, its logical conclusions weren't arrived at. The lessons that the book brought to mind were not expressed openly and completely. Consequently, I think some people would have been left with the wrong impression. But lo and behold he did write the final chapter, not within the book itself but in *Ebony* magazine under the front cover heading "The Second Reconstruction: Is History Repeating Itself?"

He titled the article, "The Second Time Around. Will History Repeat Itself and Rob Blacks of the Gains of 1960s?" So he's dealing with the issue again. We gained it [freedom] once and we lost it. Is there any law in the universe that says that we will not lose it again? He introduced the topic:

OVER.

It was, at long last, over and done with. How could anyone doubt it? How could anyone fail to see that the race problem had been solved forever?

One man who had no doubt said, "All distinctions founded upon race or color have been forever abolished in the United States."

Another who saw things this way said the category of race has been abolished by law and that "there [were] no more colored people in this country."

Thus spoke the dreamers and the prophets — and victims — in the first Reconstruction of the 1860s and the 1870s.

I don't think I have to elaborate on this kind of attitude. We run into too many youngsters today who say, "Oh, that was in slavery time. Oh, those were things we talked in the 1960s and 70s; we're in a new day now." We're not in a new day, ladies and gentlemen. The same words that we are saying today are the same words that people were saying over 100 years ago. Why are we in a new day saying the same thing that someone said 100 years ago? Bennett goes on to say:

> And it is worth emphasizing here, at the very beginning, that these flights into fantasy were based on the same "hard" facts that grip the imagination of Blacks in the second Reconstruction of the 1960s and 1970s. There was, for example, a Black man in the U.S. Senate in the 1870s and there was a Black governor in Louisiana. In the 1860s and the 1870s — as in the 1960s and 1970s — there were Black sheriffs and mayors in the South and there was open speculation about a Black vice presidential candidate. [So the Jesse Jackson run is not new in Black American history].
>
> There was, moreover, a network of civil rights laws that seemed to settle the issue *beyond* all possibility of dispute or recall. (Emphasis mine)

There are so many of us who believe that fair housing laws, anti-discrimination laws, civil rights laws, voting laws and so forth, guarantee our freedom. That is an illusion. What a flight into fantasy!

Laws are no stronger than their enforcers. The same people who pass those laws are the same people who are responsible for enforcing them. If the people who enforce the laws no longer decide to do so, the laws are of no value and have no power. Ultimately, then, fairness rests not in laws but in the activities of people and in the attitude and consciousness of people. Therefore, if the people who are responsible for enforcing those laws change their attitudes then the treatment of those people whose freedom is protected by those so-called laws is changed as well.

We cannot put our faith in White man's law and the laws enforced by Whites. I have warned and it bears repeating that if there comes a day when the society has to make a choice between feeding White children and feeding Black children, no amount of civil rights laws or any other laws on the books will prevent those people from feeding their children first. It is a silly faith we have in laws. For Black people in the 1970s, 1980s and 1990s to still rest their freedom on the basis of laws when history itself shows us that this cannot be done, we must question our sanity and what we have learned from the study of our history.

> Back there, 100 years ago there was a federal law protecting voting rights in the South — Does this all sound vaguely familiar? — and there was a national public accommodations act.

So the public accommodations law didn't begin with the freedom rides in the 1960s. We had those rights in the 1860s and 1870s as well.

> Such, in broad outline, was the racial situation 100 years ago — in the 1860s and 1870s — when racism was "forever abolished" in America for the first time.
>   It was a short "forever."

I'll just read other selected excerpts from Bennett's article.

> As almost every schoolboy knows, the first Reconstruction ended in a major historical catastrophe that wiped out the gains of the 1860s. As a consequence, *it required 100 years and oceans of blood for Black people to climb back up to the political plateau they had occupied in 1860-70.*

So, as I stated earlier, history contains both progress and regress. However, regressing at this point in history will not be a situation where we will be able to fight the battle all over again. Regressing at this point in history essentially spells annihilation for Afrikans, not only in America but for Afrikans the world over.

> For as I said in *Black Power U.S.A.*, and as DuBois said before me in *Black Reconstruction*, "Reconstruction in all of its various

11

facets was the supreme lesson for America, the right reading of which might still mark a turning point in our history."

The election of Black mayors and governors and our getting jobs in White corporations can in no way ensure the survival of Black people. We cannot make the progress of Black people synonymous with our qualifying for degrees and our getting jobs downtown. We must wake up to this because we've had this game played upon us before. Lerone Bennett mentions the founding of,

>...a prototypical War on Poverty [from the 1860s-1870s] (the Freedman's Bureau) and putting on the books civil rights laws which were in some instances stronger than civil laws passed in the 1960s and 1970s. In the wake of these events, there was an explosive growth in Black consciousness, and Blacks made many gains which surpassed, in many instances, the political gains Blacks made in the 1960s and 1970s.
>
> * * * *
>
> At one time, in fact, Black legislators were in the majority in the South Carolina legislature. In the same period, as in the comparable period in the 1960s and 1970s, poor Whites received social and economic benefits rich Whites had denied them.

Once we got in we were even good to poor White-folks. We set up school systems and whole lot of other things.[b] I'll conclude this portion by reading this:

>Long discussions about the morals and educational equivocations of Blacks obscure the main point — power or the lack of power. The worst thing that can be said about some leaders of the Reconstruction period is that they did not seem to understand that the only issue was power.

We don't talk about that issue very much today either; it seems to frighten many of us.

One final point is relevant to an understanding of the power realities of the social movements of both the first and second

Reconstructions. In both cases, social and political leaders failed to provide the economic ballots that made political ballots viable.

No one understood this better than the Black masses of the 1860s who said in marches and demonstrations that their freedom was not secure without a firm economic foundation.

Therefore, think again when we celebrate Frederick Douglass, Harriet Tubman, King, and others. We should begin to look at the central issues. If our study of Black history is merely an exercise in feeling good about ourselves, then we will die feeling good. We must look at the lessons that history teaches us. We must understand the tremendous value of the study of history for the *re-gaining* of power. If our education is not about gaining real power, we are being miseducated and misled and we will die "educated" and misled.

Why Study History

The study of history cannot be a mere celebration of those who struggled on our behalf. We must be instructed by history and should transform history into concrete reality, into planning and development, into the construction of power and the ability to ensure our survival as a people. If not, Black History Month becomes an exercise in the inflation of egos; it becomes an exercise that cuts us further off from reality. Ironically, we now see even other people who are not our friends joining us in this celebration, which means that they must see in it some means of protecting their own interests, and see in it something that works for them, and possibly against us. If they can celebrate our history and see it as something positive, then it means that we are not using it in a revolutionary sense. They do not see our study of it as a threat to their power. If we are not studying it in a way that it is a threat to their power then we are studying it incorrectly, and our celebration of it is helping to maintain us in a state of deception. So let us make sure that we look at and study history in a light such that it advances our interests, not inflates our egos and blinds us to reality.

Now let's look at European History and what I call *Historiography and Oppression: Its Functions and Outcome*. By historiography I refer to the writing of history.

We see in many of today's newspapers and popular media that many people are complaining about the state of the study of history — the fact that it's not being studied that much in high school, or that "Western civilization" is not being studied enough. Now we see a number of universities and colleges re-instituting as a part of their core curricula the study of Western civilization. I'm sure some of us are familiar with the controversies that are going on because the feminist movement is saying that feminist history should be interjected into the study of so-called Western civilization. Of course, Afrikan history advocates are also demanding that Afrikan history and non-Western civilizations be included in this area.

Sociopolitical Role of Historiography

We have an issue here that I call the *projection and image of history*. History has been down-played in this society. History has a poor reputation; often it is looked upon by too many people as essentially a set of dates and events. People ask: "Why should I study these dates; why should I study these events; what does it have to do with today?" It is as if they say, "OK, it may be used to explain how some things came about in today's world, but probably we could live without it." Often history — among even many of our people — even so-called Black History itself, has been looked upon as irrelevant and unprofitable. The idea is, "Why study Black History; it's not going to make me any money? It's not going to get me a job; what can you do with it? You should get yourself a degree in computer science; get yourself a trade. I'm not interested in Black Power; I'm interested in Green Power." These statements express foolish concepts. When we hear them we recognize that the individual has not seen the connection between history, power and money. There is a direct connection between history and economics.

I often say in this regard that if there were not a direct relationship between history and money, a direct relationship between history and power, history and rulership, history and domination, then why is it that the European *re*wrote history? Why is it that the European wants to take our history away from us? Why is it that the European wants to *re*write our history and distort it? Why is it that he doesn't want to present it at all? Apparently the rewriting, the distortion and the stealing of our history must serve vital economic, political and social functions for the European, or else he would not bother and try so hard to keep our history away from us, and to distort it in our own minds. Let us meditate on these issues and I think we'll come to realize that there is a direct relationship between history and economics, political and social development.

History and Psychology

History is projected in this culture as being irrelevant, I don't think by accident. Again, if it is made to look irrelevant, if it is made to look unprofitable, then making it appear so must serve some profitable purpose. When courses in college or university are apparently presented "nonpolitically," "objectively," "neutrally," they are actually presented in the most political way. We must understand that it is in the nature of this racist culture to hide its political agenda. Therefore, it presents so-called facts and information as if they have no political connections or implications.

I often try to show how making something political creates knowledge and information that can be of great value. I often use the concept of the "Skinner rat" to show how that concept is presented "nonpolitically" in the psychology of learning: how the rat is put in a box and can only eat if it performs a particular behavior. So if it pushes a lever — it is only as a result of pushing that lever — that it is allowed to eat. The experimenter determines when this rat is going to eat, when it is going to drink; he determines the living conditions under which this rat must survive. The rat becomes conditioned and changes as a result of the fact that the man has control of vital things in its life. Thus, we can present this paradigm in a very sterile way, in terms of learning and reinforcement principles. We can write a whole book about them, with graphs, arcane language and the whole bit.

I often point out how a Black student can learn Skinnerian psychology better than a White student and still as a result of having learned it be made dumb by it. Because, it is taught on a "race neutral," nonpolitical level. But I often ask my students whether there is only one way of looking at this situation. Why not look at it politically? This rat is conditioned; i.e., it reflects the conditions under which it is forced to survive as the result of a set of power relations. So why not analyze this experiment in terms of power relations? Based on these terms we may reach the conclusion that the conditioned rat is socially created; its personality is a social creation. What it learns is the result of a power differential between the rat and the experimenter, because the experimenter has power over the rat and uses that power to transform and create something new in the rat.

As a result of the conditioning experiment the rat is different from other unconditioned rats. It shows the effects of its conditioning. The experimenter is able to do this because the experimenter has control over the rat's circumstances. If we will go further and identify with the rat we then begin to learn something about ourselves — something of value. We will then have grasped something that can lay the foundation for revolution and change; not a sterile bit of knowledge and information that we can't use.

I've often asked my students: "Who has control of your food? Who has control of your electricity? Who has control of your water? Of your jobs? Who tells you what to wear when you go to work? Who tells you when to come to work...when to leave...when to go to lunch...how to speak...how to write...how to do this...how to do that...and how are these things taught, and how they are conditioned?"— It is by reward and punishment. "You do this you get paid; you don't do this you don't get paid; you get a raise, you get docked." What do we have here? We see the same basic situation and the same basic principles for conditioning rats are now transferred to life and reality itself. Therefore, to live in the "ghetto" under the power of another people is to be created by that people. To be rewarded or punished by that people is to be created by that people. What would happen if these "ghettos" we live in today are surrounded by a force that blocks the food and the water, cuts off the electricity and the other things? What kind of situation would we be in? But even with the water coming in, the food coming in, we are still created and conditioned by the circumstances under which we live. We are living under them as the result of the exercise of the power of another people over us. Therefore, if we wish to change this situation (i.e., the conditions under which we live), then we must change the power relationships. If we are to prevent ourselves from being created by another people and are to engage in the act of self-creation, then we must change the power relations.

With the political approach to Skinner's rat the Afrikan student not only learns what the White student learns, but learns more and learns something of value to himself. What he learns becomes a basis for self-understanding and knowledge, a plan for the future and a means by which he or she can change his or her situation. Without the lesson being taught in this way we will have a bunch of educated people who wonder why we cannot get out of the condition that we are in. We thus produce a bunch of educated people, as I have expressed before, who, the more degrees they get in business administration the fewer businesses they have to administer; who, as they go into the colleges and the Wharton Schools of Finance and the Harvard Schools of Finance, etc. find their communities being inundated by Asians and other groups. Apparently their degrees are not designed for them to control their own economic situations and circumstances. But because the information in the courses in economics are seen as "neutral" and "non-political," the student is more radically politicized than in any other way.

Afrikan-centered education recognizes that the whole of human life is a political system and, therefore, it interprets its materials politically. It is through political, economic and military action that we must change our circumstances. If those things are not applied in the context of our education then we are being educated just to be servants — educated servants! Because it is the intention of Europeans that Blacks never escape their condition of servitude. A higher education means that we will just be educated servants — nothing more, nothing less.

Hence, we have to look at our situation politically and socially.

So when history is projected as irrelevant, as unprofitable, as a system of dates and events, as a system of rarified causes and effects, it is projected that way, I think, because it helps to maintain the political and social status quo, and because it serves a politicoeconomic function. People who are ahistorical, who have little knowledge of history, are people who are more gullible, more easily manipulated and people who can be more easily adapted to the capitalist machine than people who are historically knowledgeable. History can become a basis for self-criticism, a basis for self-understanding, and more importantly, the basis for the understanding of the motives and the psychology of others. When history is not taught appropriately we are left to just follow orders, and to just trudge to our work, our jobs, without knowing the reasons why. Yet trudging to our jobs has not secured our futures at all. We must recognize that merely going to work, merely studying computer science, merely going to the office, is not enough. We are going to have to understand the psychology of the people who run this world.

We can only understand our oppressors' psychology by understanding their history. They rob us of a knowledge of history and want us to think that history is irrelevant and unimportant so that we cannot see through their deadly games. We must recognize that history is at the very center of life. As I go on I will indeed try to demonstrate more profoundly the relationship between history and life itself.

Because European history often is seen as unworthy of study in many high schools and is not at the center of the high school educational curriculum, how much more so are we, as Afrikans, tempted to see Afrikan history as unworthy. We usually take our cue from Europeans: "If they're not studying much history and their kids don't care about history then why should ours care about it? If they say it's not relevant, then how relevant can our own history be?" Watch out!

I will show that our ignorance of our history has a different outcome from the Europeans' ignorance of their history. We must also recognize that history is not only written in books, but that history is contained in every facet of life. We are interacting in the context of history right at this very moment. This church, this building is a historical event and represents historical evolution, and inside this historical structure people's minds and bodies are changed and created. History is everywhere written in the streets that we walk down, in every building, in every highway, in every yard, everywhere we go it's there; it's shaping; it's transforming; it's creating; it's blocking; it's constructing. So even though the European may stop reading his history in the books, the history of the European is still "fine and dandy" and operating everywhere we turn and every place we go. In fact, one of the reasons why it may have been reduced in terms of history books per se is because it is hidden everywhere else. It is inextricably linked and wrapped into every situation, circumstance and event of life. We study math and we would think it originated in Greece. It is usually introduced that way. We get the Pythagorean theories and Euclidean geometry and Boolean algebra and other European names spread throughout mathematics. The names and the concepts and who "first" discovered it are *history*; images being projected. We're not learning just neutral science and mathematics; European history is inculcated right in their study.

Every course we go into is intertwined with European history. We can't escape it. So simply because we don't show up in some class that calls itself the History of Europe, don't think we're escaping European history. Not by a long shot. In every discipline we study in the college/university/school we're going to run into European history: it is intimately intertwined with all disciplines.

As long as our own history is not intimately and inextricably entwined with everything we do, with every study we undertake, is not represented in our Universe, in our buildings and on our walls, in our houses and on our streets, then we need to study history more consciously than do the Europeans! We cannot always follow the route of European people. They build history in the books and then they build it into the world, or vice-versa. They may reduce their attention to the book, but history is still there and still functioning in the world. Therefore, we must forget about what the Europeans are doing and how Europeans are studying or not studying history, because we are not in their situation. Therefore doing things their way leads to injurious and different outcomes for us.

History as Psychohistory

We should look at history, more accurately, as Psychohistory, *i.e., the psychological result of undergoing certain historical experiences.* We, as individuals, are our history. I'll show later on that history is not that which is forgotten and left behind. We don't leave history behind. History is the present, history is the future. Those of us who are Afrocentric and mystical must know that the division of past, present and future is false, Eurocentric and political. The world is not a linear structure. Past, present and future are one and the same. When we have been made to believe that the past is separate and in some straight line with the future then we've already been brainwashed and set up. Our past never forgets us and is never left behind.

If you forgot your past you would not be able to understand me right now. You would not be able to walk or talk. You did not learn to walk, talk and do the things you're doing at the moment you entered here; you learned to do them in the past. Forget that then! Since that is history, leave that behind. You will see that you also have no future! Past, present and future are one, and that proposition is at the center of an Afrikan-centered history and approach.

As men with their knowledge and desire ultimately make history, so does history make men.

This is quoted from Joel Kovel's *White Racism: A Psychohistory*. When we go to see a psychiatrist, psychologist, social worker or psychotherapist, one of the first things they do is to take a so-called *case history*. They recognize that they cannot appropriately understand us as individuals unless they understand something about our unique experience as individuals. They cannot take the history and experience of another person and apply exclusively the psychology that flows from that history and experience and accurately describe you as an individual and person. That's why each person that walks through the door of helping-professionals must provide his or her own case history, and must be dealt with in terms of his or her own case history.

The same thing is true about a people. We cannot take the psychology of Europeans — and often I've stated this as a rationale for my writing of the book, *The Developmental Psychology of the Black Child*, which is based upon their history and experience, upon their values and their goals — and apply it unmodified to ourselves. This leads to misunderstanding and misdirection. One of the major problems I often point out in this context, in the area of education, is that we have a situation where the educational psychology that's taught to teachers and others who are in charge of our children is a psychology based on the history and experience of another people, and despite the best intentions of these educators they will miseducate our children in terms of that psychology.

To a very great extent the problem with the education of Black children, the crack epidemic and all of these other things we complain about day in and day out, are the result of a psychology that flows from a particular type of historical experience.

We have a school system that is based upon the psychology of White children and White people. We are trying to educate our children in that system; they are bound to fail. The very structure of the educational system itself is based upon a White model and therefore it has a built-in failure mechanism for us, one way or the other.

We must develop a psychology of our children based upon our own history and experience. It is only then that our pedagogical and educational approaches will be in line with their personalities. Only then can we move our children forward to fulfill our needs and our desires as a people. If we wish to understand ourselves and wish to understand other people's psychology we must then understand our history and their history. We must be very clear about this matter.

For us to come to understand ourselves as individual units we must ultimately come to understand not only our own personal history and experience but the history and experience of our people, since they overlap and are connected. Therefore, it is through studying the history of our people that we come to understand ourselves as individuals and as a people.

Although each person in a society is unique in the detail and fine structure of his/her life, all members of that society share certain common styles of action or ways of knowing. In other words, to the degree that we share history and experience, we share common styles of thinking and knowing. There is no such thing as an "individual" in the absolute sense of the word.

Language and Power

When we get ready to create revolution we must *re*define the world, and *re*define words; there's no way around it. In Genesis, we see Adam being given the power to name things. Through being given the power to name things he is given dominion. There is a connection between naming and dominion, between naming and bringing into reality. When we permit another people to name and define, we permit another people to gain dominion and control over us.

The languages that people learn and speak are most frequently directly related to the power relations between them. Many people will now learn Japanese, as for a while they learned Russian, as for a while they learned German, Latin, etc. Why? Because the people who speak or spoke those languages were or are in ascendance or in power at that or this time. There is no "good" English or "bad" English, or "good" language or "bad" language; there is language that's connected to power. People tend to learn first after their native tongue, whatever language is spoken by the people in power. There's a connection between the capacity to have other people speak your language and to call things by the names you give them, and power. If we wish to assume power then we must assume the capacity to name and define things.

The psychology of a culture is to a great extent a symbolic precipitant of the kinds of experiences forced upon a group of people by their history. We must recognize the intimate relationship between culture, history and personality. If we do not know our history then we do not know our personality. And if the only history we know is other people's history then our personality has been created by that history.

We must recognize this in the case of European history. It is not so much that we know European history (because 90 percent of us don't know European history and have not read it), but that we are left with some image of it, some residue of it — that we have a sense of it — is all the hegemonic European needs to begin to dominate and to control non-European peoples.

History as Mythology

I'm going to look briefly at European history as mythology, as propaganda, and as the creator of personality (which it is). It is mythology. European mythology (European hallucination) can only work against us where there is an absence of contact with reality, an absence of knowledge of Afrikan history. We hallucinate every night. These hallucinations are called dreams, and they occur at the point where we become detached from reality. We maintain our mental balance and sense of self by the input of our senses. It is necessary that for human beings to maintain sanity that they receive random input (and changing input) from the world. That is why we suffer so much when we are put into solitary confinement — where we can't see or hear anything — we may begin to have visions and hallucinations as a result thereof. There are what we call *desensitization experiments*. Some of us might have gotten a chance to see the movie, *Altered States*, that speaks to this kind of experience where when you remove a person's capacity to see, feel, hear, touch and so forth, very peculiar things happen to the mind. Hallucinations begin to occur, orientation is lost. The individual becomes imbalanced because the information that's normally used to maintain mental equilibrium is absent. We're in a similar state when we are asleep and the mind creates its own reality, its own movie show, and we watch it throughout the night. Often we don't know that we are in an unreal world until we wake up the next morning.

Mythology and hallucinations, such as those European history represents, can take us where it has taken us only as the result of the fact that we are not in touch with reality, not in touch with our Afrikan history in a realistic sense. European history is written in such a way, or projected in such a way, that we become detached and disconnected from the reality that maintains our sanity, maintains our balance and orientation. We then can fall victim to created visions and hallucinations, delusions and illusions.

In the final analysis, European history's principal function is to first separate us from the reality of ourselves and separate us from the reality of the world; to separate us from the reality of our history and to separate us from its ramifications. We will then take the hallucinations which result from these separations as representing what is real. That is its primary function — as mythology.

From the first day a reporter asked the first tough question of a government official, there has been a debate about whether government has the right to lie. It does. And in certain circumstances, government not only has the right but a positive obligation to lie.

This is stated by Jody Powell (who served under former President Jimmy Carter, as press secretary) in his book, *The Other Side of the Story*. A very interesting admission. Many have heard me say that Europeans, who comprise 10 percent of the world's population, can only rule over the 90 percent by lying, by deceit and force. The only way that we can be in the condition we are in, as a people, is to believe lies. Our mentality has been reversed and our behavior made backwards because we take the lie for the truth, and the truth for the lie. A small minority in the world can only rule by making backwards the mentality of the large majority. It makes mentally backward the large majority by reversing the truth, creating lies and getting the majority to believe the lies that it creates. Powell has honestly admitted it.

European historiography lies in many ways. It even lies when ostensibly telling the truth. An effective propagandist doesn't want to tell too many big lies, too many obvious lies; he wants to tell the truth in a sort of way that gets him where he wants to go.

We have to recognize that European history-writing is an institution the way any other discipline is an institution. And the function of institutions in any oppressive society is to maintain the status quo. I don't care what institution we may talk about; whether we talk about the family institution, the criminal justice institution, the economic institution, the religious institutions, the health establishment, the educational institutions; they all have one thing in common in a Eurocentric oppressive system — to maintain the status quo and to maintain Afrikan people in oppression. We must keep this in mind. It is not so much what they say or don't say they represent. It is how they function that is of importance. The European writing of history is in tandem with everything else European and its purpose is ultimately the same: to maintain European power and domination.

European historiography does this by a number of means. It may do this by the pure falsification and concealment of history, by omission and by commission. It may do it by what I call a "theft of history." We, in studying Egyptology, are trying to take back what European historiography has stolen, completely falsified; to erase the new false identities it placed on the Afrikan Egyptian people. Or when there isn't a direct lie we get a history book that's written about Egyptians without any reference to ethnicity. We have an unwritten rule which says that if ethnicity is not mentioned then we are talking about White-folks. That rule has been so deeply ingrained within us that we can read history about ourselves in great detail but project *whiteness* right into it and "whitewash" our own identity.

We have been set-up by Eurocentric historiography in such a way that when the word "slave" is mentioned we assume that they are talking about us, Afrikan people. So we read about slaves in history and right away assume they must be talking about "colored" folks. As if no other people has ever been enslaved but Black people. In other words, historiography can create an outright lie (as it often does), or present itself "neutrally", "non-ethnically", and achieve deceptive ends since it has already set us up to misperceive reality and truth. The European historiography so "beautifully" sets us up that we *supply* the lie while looking directly at truth.

This society gets away by pretending that it is free and open. Ladies and gentlemen, it does provide tremendous amounts of information and puts that information right in our neighborhoods, right before our eyes; we're just overrun with information. There's so much information in libraries until one young man went into one and just by reading found out how to develop an atomic bomb...the mechanism, the whole thing...not from classified data, but data right on the library shelves. He had to have intentions and needs to do that, didn't he? He had to have goals, values, other things that took him to those books; and those mental structures allowed him to pull out the relevant information and piece it together. Without appropriate motivational structures information can be put right before our faces and we will gain nothing from it.

So we're in the situation, as Black people, where the information is put right before our faces and we gain relatively little from it. It can only be put before our faces the way it is because we have been so mentally and motivationally structured that we will not and cannot take that information and transform it to our own advantage. Therefore, this country talks about

...freedom of information! "See, we let them read anything." But it goes back to the phrase: *The best way to hide anything from a Negro is to put it in writing.*

Historiography may function as *propaganda* — propaganda being an effort to persuade people to a point of view on an issue. History can be used to intimidate. European achievements are inflated and the next thing we know, we are asking ourselves "How we can fight this great people?" We've been frightened! They talk about the great discoveries they've made and we say to ourselves, "Hey, we'd better hang in with these people because if we lose them we're going back to the Dark Ages." We think this way because they've destroyed our confidence, our capacity to think for ourselves and to believe that we are capable of creating a world as great or greater than the Eurocentric one that presently exists. In this way European historiography functions to maintain a social system, to "psychologize" and create a personality orientation in its readers or hearers.

Even if we forget every fact and detail of inflated Eurocentric history, its intimidatory impression stays with us even when the content is lost. That's the point of it, to leave the impression, because that impression will become a dynamic source of behavioral orientation toward the world.

The European doesn't care whether or not we remember the facts and the details as long as we just remember the impression, as long as our personalities have been impressed and transformed in a fashion compatible with European interests. Historiography may be used and function to rationalize ideology and justify the status quo, to motivate activity and to create consciousness. We see that all the time, the rationalization of slavery through the use of history, the rationalization of European domination through the use of history. Why is our cultural history stolen from us? So that we can think that we had no culture until the European gave us his, or projected his own upon us; so that we can feel that we are not capable of culture, and of developing a culture of our own, one that could be respected the world over; so that we develop an inferiority complex and the other kinds of complexes we talk about so often today.

When you steal a people's history you can justify ruling over them and thus justify domination. More importantly, history may be used to influence personality, culture, roles, and to motivate us to commit suicide, to provoke us to commit *menticide*[1] and may be used to create or rationalize fratricide, genocide and self-destruction.

How many times have we, maybe in our own personal lives, attacked someone because we were given the wrong history about them? How many murders have been perpetrated because someone believed a lie? How many wars have been started because the population was lied to and a history projected in such a way that it motivated them to kill? A bogus, thoroughly wrongful fabrication can lead one to imprisonment, can lead one to murder, or lead to wars, or to being killed and destroyed. So there is a direct connection between history and the way people behave and act, between what one thinks of as history and killing, death, destruction and imprisonment.

So history is no casual thing that one picks up while passing through school. It becomes a part of one's total orientation toward the world. If it were not, why then does the European see himself as the sole, valid historian in the world and tries to see himself as the only one who should determine what history is? We are, to a very great extent, what we are today as people as the result of believing lies presented as truth. We must recognize that this often comes in the guise of history.

Eurocentric history most popularly functions as mythology. Mythology has many functions. We can't go into them here today due to constraints of time. Mythology often can be seen as a form of denial of reality. If a memory is too painful to be recalled, if recalling it means suffering, pain, shame, guilt and other negative things, the individual may not only deny the reality of that memory and experience but may actually creat

---

[1] A term coined by Dr. Bobby Wright to explain the mental genocide practiced against Afrikan people.

a mythology in their places. By becoming obsessed and caught up in that mythology, he uses it as a means of keeping out of his conscious memory the traumatic experiences that he fears.

The European must undoubtedly fear the truth of Afrikan history. Recall the phrase: *Ye shall know the truth and the truth shall make you free.* And if we are not free today, then we must not know the truth. If Eurocentric history and other disciplines are true then why aren't we free? The knowledge of truth threatens those who wish to imprison us, keep us imprisoned, and keep us dominated. The projection of the European version of history into our minds as mythology is a way of repressing truth within our own minds and within our breasts as a people.

European historiography functions to maintain repression. Often, the person represses painful information that threatens his equilibrium because he may be profiting by the lies he tells himself and others. The European profits by the lies he tells, the false perceptions and consciousness he creates in himself and others. Therefore, truth and a more realistic history threatens these gains. His self-esteem and vision of who he is and what he is, is maintained through the projection of his history as mythology. That's one of the functions of mythology — to maintain self-esteem.

The European projection of history not only serves to drive out and repress truth, but also to maintain the inflated European ego. Therefore, truthful history is not only seen as a correction of his history, but as a direct attack against his ego, status and position in the world. That's why Afrikan-centered history is reacted to with such great anxiety. That's why almost anything Afrikan is reacted to with alarm. But it is only through *Afrikan*ess, only through the projection of the truth of Afrikaness, that our freedom can be attained as a people, and European domination brought to an end.

Whether a mythology is perceived as true or false is sociologically unimportant. Some Blacks would debate Elijah Muhammad's view of the world, about the White man being the Devil. Of course, the "negro" who doesn't want to do anything gets into the fine points of that. He's very careful to distinguish the good ones from the bad ones and the ones in-between. He has

29

a graduated measuring rod; he works them out by degrees. But when the White man enforced segregation down South, the good Black-folk and the bad Black-folk sat right in the back of the bus; it didn't matter. The mythology didn't differentiate: "You're black; get back." That's the deal; you're bad. The function was not that of telling truth. The idea was how that mythology (i.e. all Blacks are bad) helped maintain the racial status quo. The idea is not whether Whites are Devils or Angels, but what would happen if we dealt with Whites as if they were Devils. How would that transform our situation as a people? How would that transform our behavior as a people? Would it move us closer to doing for self, would it move us closer to controlling our destinies, our own behaviors, gaining control of our economies and our nations? Would it remove us from being manipulated and used by another system? It is not about truth alone; it is about self-control. It is about the gaining of power. It is about being able to protect and advance our survival. But if we get caught up in the minutiae of trying to figure out whether there are good ones and bad ones and others in between, we may find ourselves being destroyed in our studies. That's why we have to recognize that the Honorable Elijah Muhammad was the greatest psychologist we ever had, and many of us still have not come to understand that yet. Some of us thought that we were doing our "intellectual thing" when we got caught up trying to point out his "mythologies." Not at all; we must look at function.

So European history, whether it is true to the extent and/or in the context within which it is projected, or whether it is false, is really not the ultimate point. It's the fact that it functions as a mythology, and as mythology it functions to maintain European power, domination, and control. It is our attack against it as a mythology that we must be concerned with as an Afrikan people. Because the mythology becomes a part of our mental structure. It is used as a tool of intellection, a tool of comprehension, a tool of dealing with the world and relating to the world. A mythology organizes the world, organizes behavior; it organizes interpersonal and intergroup relations. Whatever mythology we believe is one that organizes our approach to other people, our perception of ourselves and of other people. It provides answers. The answers may not be right, they may be wrong; but it still provides an answer. And that's psychologically satisfying. Nothing threatens us and nothing upsets us like unanswered questions. Often Man projects a mythology in order to get himself out of his agony of dealing with unanswered questions and to put his mind at rest.

We have to recognize the function of mythology since mythology seeks to mold character and to motivate, as well as to de-motivate. Mythology often takes control of the domain of discourse, in the sense that just the presentation of European history — leaving Afrikan history aside — implies that Afrikan history is not worth learning. I often tell college students that "you look at your college catalog and you see a course in there and assume that because it's in the catalog it's worth learning." You say to yourself, "If it's not there then it must not be worth learning; because if it was worth learning it would be there." You look at the list of required courses and you don't see anything about your history as being *required*. You assume that the most important courses are required and since the ones related to us are not required then they must not be important. Just the reading of the catalog inflates one group and deflates the other. It creates a superiority complex in one and an inferiority complex in the other. When we name things, when we speak of things in order to exclude contrary truths, we create and uncreate reality. This is the role that European historiography has arrogated to itself.

History and Societal Amnesia

History is a time dimension. History structures time. I frequently try to point out that culture is not only about behavior, dress and so forth, but that all cultures have a time dimension related to them. I talk about this relative to the education of our children to indicate that our children are often flunked and destroyed by the time structure of the schools they attend. Who told us that classes only have to last 45 minutes?

"Oh, the White-folks teach theirs 45 minutes." But that, apparently, is a time system that's connected to and works for them, that is in someway intimately connected to their history and experience.

When we look at ourselves, are we going to tell ourselves that our children are destroyed by the aftereffects of our enslavement, jim crowism, miseducation, poor self-image, all the other things we moan and groan about and yet we don't make time in a curriculum for instructing them so as to remove these obstacles to learning? If not then, we will destroy them. Therefore, our time system for teaching our children cannot be a duplicate of the European time system. We must recognize there's a time dimension related to our history and ourselves as a people. In knowing our history we get to know our time dimension, we get to know how much time has to be dedicated to various tasks if we are to achieve what we need to achieve. Forget about other people's time. Who gives a hoot about whether our children are reading ahead or behind White children? Who told us they had to read the same thing, at the same time, at the same age? If they have a different history, a different experience, different goals and different ways, then doesn't it stand to reason that they may be achieving different milestones at different times? But it's the very fact that we try to impose the time system of another people upon our children that creates the so-called deviations we complain about so much, and our children are destroyed in the process.

So when we let another people write history — and history is an arbitrary division of time — they define us within that division of time. So we see European history talking about "World War I", "World War II", etc. That's not the only way to divide up time, in terms of wars. No! We have been at war with the European continuously for the last 2,000 years — a non-stop war. But when we internalize European divisions of time, it takes us away from our own history and from understanding our own adversarial relationship with them and other people, and takes us completely outside of ourselves. Therefore, history as mythology, even if it tells the truth, by the very fact of its structuring of time can still be used as propaganda, to manipulate, and create unreality in consciousness.

European history to a considerable degree, attempts to control consciousness by the way it is presented. We saw a movie called *The Birth of A Nation.* Why not the "Death of a Nation?" Indigenous American (so-called Indian) nations existed at the time. At the same time we speak of the "birth" of some nations, other nations were dying. But we are focused on their so-called birth. Even more pernicious than this is the fact that many of our people feel as if they do not come into existence and self-consciousness until they have been recognized by European historians. So Columbus "discovers" America and it's almost as if the "Indian" comes into reality and into self-consciousness as the result of Columbus' discovery. Before that time they were nothing. Dead! And many of us still have that deep psychology, that we are "invisible" people until White-folks recognize that we exist. It's a heavy psychology that rules us today; we are not famous until they make us famous; we are not anything until they make us something. Before that we are nothing.

History as propaganda, history as mythology, creates and brings into consciousness. History by Europeans is seen as a validation of truth. It establishes authority. It's a puzzling situation, as I've often pointed out to my students, that we use as arbiters of truth those who have lied to us most. These are the kinds of contradictions that keep us crazy, and they are widespread. Consequently, we can only feel it is truth when it comes out of a European historical mouth — solely.

Consequences of Historical Amnesia

In the interest of time I'll just end my analysis of European history and look a bit at another issue. I'm really more concerned about what happens when we don't know or forget our history. Eurocentric history is used to motivate forgetting in the Afrikan personality, to create amnesia, to maintain repression. Many of us, as individuals, seek to forget our history and do not want to confront our history because of the anxiety, the anger, the fear, the shame, the guilt we feel when we read about some aspects of the Afrikan experience, and hence will often stay away from it. We think we have escaped its effects thereby. We can hear some of our uninformed children say, "Well, that was back there 100 years ago; that ain't got nothing to do with me today." The Black child at this very moment is still affected and suffering from the slave experience, whether he or she knows it or not. In fact, as Russell Jacoby says in his book, *Social Amnesia*:

> Exactly because the past is forgotten, it rules unchallenged. To be transcended it must first be remembered. Social amnesia is society's repression of remembrance.

Simply because we choose to forget a traumatic event, simply because we choose not to learn of a traumatic history and a history that may make us feel ashamed, does not mean that that history is not controlling our behavior. Simply because we don't know our history, and may have not heard of it, does not mean that the history does not control our behavior.

One of the most profound things that we've learned in psychology is that the most powerful forces that shape human behavior are those factors that are consciously *not* remembered by human beings, that are unknown by the person, are those experiences the individual can swear he's never had. That is one of the paradoxes of human behavior, that the very things that shape us and make us behave the way we do, see the world the way we see it and relate to people the way we relate to them, are those things that occurred in our lives at points we cannot remember or recall.

The personality is in part shaped in the womb itself; shaped by the genes, shaped in part by the birth process itself; shaped in the very first two years of life. Yet very few, if any of us can remember in detail those first two years of life. Yet it is those very first two years that determine our behavior from "8 to 80". And so the idea that we don't know, that we're not aware of certain early experiences, does not mean that we have escaped their effects. In fact it puts us more profoundly under the influence of these unknown forces.

Amnesia is a state where a person seeks unconsciously to forget aspects of his/her past life because apparently those aspects are painful and, therefore, the individual seeks to rid himself of them. Consequently, by ridding himself of his conscious remembrance of painful experiences he seeks to rid himself of anxieties and fears connected with them. He may then succeed in forgetting those experiences completely, to the point where he cannot recall them, but this does not mean that those experiences do not continue to operate within his personality.

There are those of us who are made ashamed of our history of enslavement, who are made ashamed by the distorted presentation of Afrikan history (which is why the European distorts it and presents it the way he does), are made to think that prior to slavery we were essentially culturally invisible and savage and only achieved visibility and civility when the European came on the scene. Many of us attempt to repress any knowledge of our American slave experience. But we should heed the fact that a person and people who suffer from social amnesia live lives that are determined by fear, anxiety, terror and trauma. When we attempt to escape our history because we're afraid of it, when we escape knowledge because it terrifies and makes us feel ashamed, then it is terror and fear and shame that *determine* our lives. We then live, not in terms of our reality and in terms of the integration of our reality but in terms of what we are afraid of, i.e., what we are ashamed of, what we are trying to hide, what we are trying not to confront ourselves with. Life is then lived in terms of denial, in terms of escape and addiction. Many of the murders, deaths, and much of the destruction that we see in our communities today are the result of people trying to escape history, and living their lives in terror and fear of their own history and reality. That is why I contend that history is directly related to our concrete existence; it is not something you happen to take in school. It is a part of our real lives because without it, it will make us take dope, kill, steal, and it'll make us do all kinds of terrible things because our lives are not determined by relating to history appropriately — but determined by fear.

Those people and parents who have escaped their own history as a result of trying to escape anxiety, fear, shame and so forth, may pass *escapism* onto their children as history. That history of escapism then becomes a part of their personality and they become vulnerable to addictions and all other kinds of terrible habits and orientations in the world. Why do we think we were robbed of our history if it was not to serve this purpose?

The individual who has amnesia suffers distortion of and blindness to reality. The individual who cuts himself off from his history is self-alienated. There's a whole part of himself that's completely shut off from his use. It's as if there were two parts. One part is unknown, yet because it is unknown doesn't mean that it is not effective. *We have to devote energy to unknowing.* We have to direct perception to unknowing. We have to say: "Let me turn my face so I cannot see; let me not think about it." So the struggle to not know itself becomes a creator of behavior and personality structure. So the idea that not knowing one's history somehow permits one to escape it is a lie. In fact, it brings one under the domination of the more pernicious effects of that history and opens the personality up for self-alienation, self-destruction.

A person who is suffering from amnesia lives a life based on negation, not on affirmation, not on growth and development, but lives life in such a way as to deny life and reality and to deny parts of his own personality and himself. Life then becomes a negation and is used to maintain a negation instead of life as it should be lived — as affirmation, as growth, enhancement and development. And people who live their lives as a negation live the lives that we see ourselves living today — going deeper and deeper into hell and going deeper into self-destruction as a people.

History is real; it brings real, tangible results. When we wish to negate it and not integrate it, when we wish to negate it and not affirm it, then it negates us in the end. The negation wins out. The Afrikan person who lives in social amnesia brought on by the projection of mythological Eurocentric history, lives a life that is unintegrated and misunderstood. Why is our behavior so puzzling to us? We sometimes ask ourselves, "Why did I do that? I don't know what makes me do this." Here's behavior flowing out from our own mind and personality and we *don't* know its sources. It means that we become a puzzlement to ourselves, the ones we think that we should understand best. Often, other people can understand us better than we can understand ourselves. Frequently they have a greater knowledge of the history that made us into who we are than we do.

If we don't know our history, or if we've made our history unconscious and therefore placed it out of awareness, that unconscious history becomes a source of unconscious motivation, then why we behave the way we do becomes a puzzle. We're confused by our own behavior. If we want to know why we behave the way we do then we must know our history: the unconscious must be made conscious.

Consequently, when the European makes us unconscious of our own history, we not only become unconscious of our history as knowledge, we become unconscious of the sources of our behavior as persons and as a people; and our own behavior becomes a mystery. "Why do Black-folks act like that?" We get discouraged. We give up. "We ain't gonna straighten them (i.e., Black people) out man!" Because we can't figure it out.

When history is misperceived and we look to a White Jesus and we pray to that White Jesus, then walk out and see the poverty, smell the stench, see the drugs, people holding babies up to shield themselves from bullets and all this kind of stuff ...it's not difficult for us to step over a thin line that says, "Boy, we must have done something really terrible in the past for us to be suffering the way we do; as much as we pray to Jesus, for us to be suffering the way we do." *"God must have cursed us,"* we surmise. Then we're ready for the old Ham mythology. We set ourselves up and we introject inferiority into ourselves. We take it into our breast and pass it onto our children and we are done in. This is what happens when we don't know our history and don't know the history of other people. There are some "negroes" who seek to escape their history and identity by telling themselves, "I don't see color." Well, do you think that means the world doesn't see you as "colored"? A lot of people fail to understand that because they may choose not to see something in a certain way, that other people still may choose to do so. That assertion (*I don't see color*) doesn't change the way other people look at them. In fact, this perceptual misdirection sets them up to be manipulated. Almost every day we hear "negroes" say that they have been manipulated and are being manipulated in some sort of way. In fact, they often say it to justify their being manipulated and not confronting their reality; because they don't want to deal with the realistic situation that they live in. They want to deny the European's terroristic rule on Earth, deny his evil, deny his domination over them and deny his destruction of the Earth and life itself. So they choose not to see color, so they can't see White for what it is. They use it to justify not knowing their own history and not knowing themselves because they don't see "color" — thereby maintaining the amnesia.

When we get into social amnesia — into forgetting our history — we also forget or misinterpret the history and motives of others as well as our own motives. The way to know other people is to know one's self. The way to learn of our own creation, how we came to be what we are, is getting to know ourselves. It is through getting to know the self intimately that we get to know the forces that shaped us as a self. Therefore, knowing the self becomes a knowledge of the world. A deep study of Black History is the *most* profound way to learn about the psychology of Europeans and to understand the psychology that flows from their history.

If we don't know ourselves, not only are we a puzzle to ourselves; other people are also a puzzle to us as well. We assume the wrong identity and identify ourselves with our enemies. If we don't know who we are then we are whomever somebody else tells us we are.

Changing our Name

We don't have time to talk about Jesse Jackson and his Afrikan-American campaign, and *The New York Times* which feels we are not Afrikan-American until *The New York Times* says we are Afrikan-American. I want to read this excerpt from January 31, 1989, *The New York Times:*

> A *movement* led by Jesse Jackson [which is interesting in that it is a total misinterpretation and distortion of history right there] to call Blacks African-Americans has met with both rousing approval and deep-seated skepticism in a debate that is coming to symbolize the *role* and *history* of Blacks in this country. (Emphasis added)

Even these people recognize that a name is connected to social role. A name is not just something you call people, but the name a people are called signifies their role. Therefore, a change of name represents a people's attempt to change their role and position in the world. Some "negroes" think that to change our name is just some foolish game we're playing. It's not about that. Even other people recognize that.

> This change of name — if it comes, will be deeply felt, and if what it implies becomes a true part of the Afrikan-American personality — represents fundamental changes in this world.

It is not a game we're playing here. Identity is very important, as is the idea that Black people would dare to name themselves. Whites recognize that as an incursion on their power of naming and an incursion on their power of domination.

History is what creates a shared identity in a people. It is based on that shared identity that they act collectively. To take away a people's history, to degrade their history is to degrade their sense of shared identity, is to remove the basis upon which they must behave collectively and reach their goals collectively. That's why the history is rewritten and why people get alarmed about it.

When we suffer from social amnesia we forget the debt we owe to past and future generations. We then misinterpret our accomplishments as solely our own individual achievements. I remind my college student audiences that, "you're not here in this college just because you're smart, because you come from the right family, because you scored high on the SATs and all the other stuff." Blacks have scored high on the SATs since the beginning of time; we've had good families and the right families from the beginning; we've had 4.0 students from the beginning; we had all of that and we were still kept out of the university. So you're not here because of your own personal achievement. You're here because people who didn't score anything put their bodies and their lives on the line to see that you got here — and you owe them something for that. If this institution decides to put you out, it will be these same people who will be up here to see that you get in here again! Some of you want to forget that history and then claim you owe them nothing when you make your couple of little bucks in front of a TV camera or some other place. Then not only do you forget them, you forget the ones coming after you, and you don't make sure that they can also get in and their privileges are also maintained. You want to act like *revolution* is something that's temporary and not permanent: It is permanent. You forget your history and forget who you are and lose your obligation to the past, to those who made your success possible and do not fulfill your obligations for those to come — some of whom will be your own sons and daughters!

When we suffer from social amnesia we identify with abstractions: "I am not Black; I am not Afrikan; I am a human being. I am an American." Sterile, abstract identity. The closer we get to it the less we see of it, and the more we recognize that it has no meaning. "What is that? Who is that? What does that stand for? What does it mean?" It's empty, and people who identify themselves with these abstractions are also empty and experience their lives as empty, as people who have no feelings. They identify with the abstraction so as to escape feelings. Therefore, we see them detached and cut-off from themselves as persons, as well as from their people. In fact they use their abstract identity to escape their responsibilities to their own people and to escape the pain and struggle that happens today to be a part of our situation.

I love the challenge of being Afrikan in today's world; it's wonderful! I love digging in my heels against the impossible odds of being Black in America! What greater challenge could we have in life today than to be Afrikan? What greater testament to our heroism than to overcome the problems that face us today? What greater opportunity can we have to transform ourselves and transform the world in the process? Why would we wish to escape this kind of challenge? It's too wonderful, too magnificent. We should eat this kind of challenge for breakfast!

When we become socially amnesic we forget our location in time and space, because history is about locating one's self in time and space. History is a grid, a set of coordinates that permit the individual to locate himself in reference to other points in the world. History is a mathematical concept, ladies and gentlemen, it is a geometrical concept; it locates and positions one relative to other things.

History and the Manipulation of Time

When one is shorn of one's past and does not see the direction of one's future and is very uncertain of one's present, then one cannot tell from whence one comes and where one is going, where one is — and suffers as a result. Let me quickly read in the context of history as a time dimension from a little piece done in the *Omni* magazine, February, 1984. It's called *"Timeless Minds."* It reads:

"When I awake you the past will be gone", Dr. Bernard Aaronson of the New Jersey Neuro-Psychiatric Institute, told a deeply hypnotized college student. When the posthypnotic suggestion took hold, the student became drowsy and infantile, losing both memory and the powers of speech.

The hypnotist had given the student the posthypnotic suggestion *"when I wake you the past will be gone."* He then woke the student. The student reported how he felt. He exhibited infantile behavior, losing both memory and the powers of speech. "Later he reported a vague sense of meaningless." Why am I here? What's my purpose? What's the meaning of life? — those kinds of querying and issues. A loss of history, a loss of his past was created within the student.

The young man without a past was one of the ten college students who took part in an unusual experiment with psychological time warp.

So there was a manipulation of time. A manipulation of an individual's past is a manipulation of his time dimension, a warping of his time which warps his perception, warps his experience and perception of himself. People who play with our history are playing with our sense of time, playing with our sense of place and who we are, and what we're about! So is history just an elective? No, ladies and gentlemen!

Aaronson gave some subjects posthypnotic suggestions that eliminated their past, present, or future; he gave others a vastly expanded past, present, or future. The consequences were profound.

With no future, people feel a loss of identity and a euphoric, mystical sensation, free of both anxiety and motivation. One student found himself "in a boundless immanent present." Expanding the future, on the other hand, canceled all fears of death and induced serenity, contemplation and a feeling of self-fulfillment.

Being robbed of a past brought on a semi-infantile torpid state, and the students with a dilated past became egocentric and inhibited.

* * * *

Canceling the present was the most disturbing however. One subject turned catatonic; others became severely depressed and almost schizophrenic. Stopping subjective time altogether produced an eerie sensation of death. "The world moves on, but I don't," one student observed.

Aaronson's conclusion:

"Life must carry some sense of direction, from past to present or present to future, to seem worth living. People given a present shorn of a past and future become preoccupied with death and behave like schizophrenics."

What are we saying here? The hypnotist, by manipulating this man's attitude toward his past manipulated his consciousness, real capacities and abilities. He just wasn't in a state of illusion; he had memory problems. He had problems getting meaning out of life. He lost his sense of purpose in life. "He became lethargic, drowsy and sleepy." *People who manipulate the past and present manipulate one's mentality, sanity, contact with reality and the ability to deal with reality.* In other words, the manipulation of history creates real effects in the individual's personality. Our history not being taught to us correctly ensures that our potential will be forever undeveloped as a people and that we will not challenge those who rule over us.

Intellectual structures and powers are undeveloped when we suffer from amnesia; they are restricted and alienated. Some of my Black students say, "Hey, I know nothing about Black History; but I know math, I know computer science, and I know this and that. So apparently it didn't do me much harm." Oh no, don't deceive yourself! Being cut off from your past only means that you have gained knowledge at the cost of being alienated, you have gained an alienated knowledge. Alienated knowledge can only be used in the interest of aliens. Look at who you work for once you know computer science and don't know your history! That's one of the unwritten rules. They will teach you math and science and so forth to the degree that you forget what and who you are — your history — and forget your connectedness with your people. Because it's only when you are unconnected that you can be of use to aliens. You cannot use alienated knowledge for yourself. Knowledge must be connected and contained in a historical structure, in a cultural structure, if it is to work for a particular people. That's why you can get degrees in business administration and build no businesses. You can be the CEO of Xerox yet you won't build your own.

History and Wealth Creation

Our resources are pillaged and our creativity is retarded when we become socially amnesic. We forget coping skills that were learned in the past and that yet can still be useful in the present. If we forget everything we've learned in the past, what babbling babies we would become. If we forget everything we've learned in the past we would not know how to cope with many of the problems and issues that confront us as we move through life. We can't drop our past; that's where we learned our coping skills.

Let me give a quick example of what this really means. Let's look at economics. Afrikan-Americans earn $300 billion per year spending-money, which would make us the *ninth* or tenth richest nation on Earth, yet we perceive ourselves as "poor." A group that can only spend money, can only support other peoples. Harlem's 125th Street now contains 68 Korean businesses; 68 and growing fast! But I don't see Koreans walking up and down those blocks spending any money at all. In fact, I hardly see any other ethnic group on that street; I only see Afrikan people. Even Hispanics are not on it to any great degree. Yet we enrich the Koreans and other ethnic groups, support them, feed their children while ours starve and die, become addicted to crack, rob and steal, and do the kind of things we do not approve of. This is a result of a people who have forgotten their history.

We say, "Well, if we had the money..." It is not money; we are not suffering from a lack of money. No way! Over $50 billion is earned and created [by Blacks] between New York and Newark, so we're not suffering from any great money problems. We're suffering from the *absence* of an economic system. Money is not a system; money is what it is. A system involves the systematic and organized utilization of money; a systematized utilization and distribution of money. Without the pattern, without the system, without the organization, one does not have an economy. An economy exists prior to money. There were economies in the world before money was invented. We don't even have to have money to have an economic system. So ultimately, when we study economic systems we recognize that an economic system at its base refers to the nature of the relationship between people. It's the systematic way people choose to relate one to the other that makes an economic system — Not money. When we lack a systematic way of relating to each other then we can have money and still be poor, have money and be robbed — which is what we are.

The Economics of Maladjustment

Why do we suffer from this problem then? Why is the Black personality created? I try to get across the fact that every maladjusted characteristic in the Black personality serves an economic function. Each maladjustive characteristic is not there by accident; it's not there simply because Europeans hate us: It's there because it maintains their economic dominance. If I've got money I can help you, but if I distrust you, I won't help you and you may not make it. It's not the absence of money...it's the presence of mistrust. If I will not cooperate, if you cannot rely on me, then we cannot have an economic system, even though we may have money. In other words, a people must trust, be reliable, be dependable, have respect for each other if they are to develop a viable economic system. When they have those kinds of relationships they have a social system, and they can build and they grow economically. Suspiciousness and other negatives are implanted in the collective Black personality so that Afrikan people cannot challenge European people, even though we are a majority of the people on this Earth and we live over the riches of this Earth.

A people who do not share history, who do not appreciate the shared experiences that their history represents, are a people who cannot utilize mutual trust, dependability, and so forth, upon which to build an economic social system. Afrikan people who forget their history are a people who forget that they had an economy before the European came into existence. They are a people who forget that their economy was developed and maintained prior to the European imperial ascendancy.

Let me quote something here about a people who didn't forget some part of their history. These are Afrikan people cited in the *New York Times*, Monday, November 30, 1987. The article is called *"Informal Capitalism Grows in Cameroon."*

— Grassroots Credit System, DOUALA, Cameroon.

When Samuel Nanci needed $35,000 to open his Joie de Vivre Bar here, he did not bother with banks. Instead he turned to the tontines, an informal credit system rooted in African tradition. Without signing a paper or filling out a form, Mr. Nanci emerged from his monthly tontine meeting with $35,000 in cash.

I tell people, there's no such thing as a Black bank.[c] There's not a Black bank in existence. There's no such animal, whether Freedom National, Carver, etc. — none of them are Black banks. Anytime you have a bank regulated by another people and by another people's rules, it's not yours; you're just there. On another occasion I'll show you where the presence of Black banks have retarded Black economic development, not advanced it. Other groups will have moved into economic existence and control before they even build a bank. After they build an economic base then you'll see them build a bank, not the other way around. But dominated people who don't know themselves do it backwards; they build a bank and don't even have anything to invest in, ignoring the fact that banks make money by loans and investments. That's why Black banks have suffered. We have to build a basic economic "mom and pop" base first. It is through lending people money this way and so forth that a banking system grows, not the other way around. But the "negro" starts with the bank first because it makes him look good. It retards us and then puts us under the rule of another people. They tell us that we can do only this, that and the other thing with our money. Let us use our money under our own rules and regulations.

Why can't we raise $35,000 and build ourselves fruit stands and build the stores we want or do something else with it? It's in our tradition. But if we suffer from amnesia this tradition is not available to us. Yet here's a people [the Cameroonians] who remember tradition, and their remembrance of their past and tradition permits them to perform economically. Who says that history is not connected with economics? Do not let anyone tell us that lie from this day on!

For years development economists saw African's tontines as archaic tribal institutions that would die out with the rise of modern economies based on European-style banking systems.

In other words, we see the European banking systems were expected to destroy native systems, which is what they have done in too many Afrikan countries. The banks are killing our creativity and capacity to use the money that we have in our pockets.

But now many economists see the tontines as a highly efficient method of promoting grassroots roots efforts in capitalism.

They cite Cameroon. In the first half of the 1980's, this Central African nation had the continent's highest average economic growth rate, 7 percent a year. Cameroonians rate of participation in tontines — 47 percent — was the highest in five French-speaking Afrikan countries surveyed by Marcomer Gallup International. By contrast, only 13 percent of the people surveyed in the five nations had savings accounts.

"Banks don't match the mentality of the people," said Theodorvet-Marie Fansi, the director of an economic consulting firm here. "They are colonial structures."

What is he saying? — That the economic system set up by Europeans does not match us. It doesn't match our mentality. Where does that mentality come from? History and experience — Tradition! The European banking system comes from another people's tradition, another people's history; it represents the means by which they have developed to deal with their own economic situation. Therefore, it doesn't fit us and our needs.

It helps when we [Afrikan Americans] look at our economic situation in terms of a developing economy. Our economic circumstance is one that requires a rather high level of what is normally called *venture capital*, high risk capital. When we deal with banks we're dealing with a system in a so-called mature economy. Therefore, the basis upon which they lend and allocate money, etc., is foreign and separated from our economic reality. That's why we get turned down again and again, besides the fact that Whites want to maintain domination. We must develop a banking system and a money system in line with our economic reality. The article makes this point where a participant in one of these "informal systems" states that:

> "I have attended tontines where the monthly pot is $1 million," said Antoine L. Ntsimi, a Cameroonian banker with a business degree from the University of Chicago. With a tontine loan, Mr. Ntsimi recently started construction of a four-story, $850,000 building that will hold offices, retail stores and apartments.

The monthly pot is worth $1 million! This is a group of people who are organized along the lines of Afrikan tradition which makes available to its members $1 million per month. Here we are, rich and filled with money and can't even make available to our own people $10 per month. That means that one person belonging to that group each month has available to him/her $1 million to do what he/she needs to get done. Did they go to banks? Did they go to the Small Business Administration? No, they went to themselves — because they were within their tradition.

The article describes a man that went into a tontine and built a hotel. He needed $835,000; he went into the tontines and got it. He's in touch with the tradition, in touch with the past. Don't tell me that our past is not connected to money; it's a lie. All people use their past to create money.

> In Cameroon bankers complain of loan delinquency rates as high as 50 percent. But tontine payments are taken so seriously that borrowers faced with delinquency have been known to commit suicide.
>
> Tontines work, economists say, because their loans are backed by *social pressure*, a system familiar to Africans. Banks perform poorly because their loans are backed by paper guarantees made to strangers, a concept alien to Africans.
>
> Tontines exist in much of sub-Saharan Africa, from Burkina Faso to Ghana to Zaire and Rwanda. But Cameroon's Bamileke

tribesmen have popularized interest-bearing tontines to such an extent that bankers complain that tontines contribute to the current crisis in banking liquidity.

In their original form, tontines allowed peasants to pool their labor rather than their money. With the introduction of the money economy in the 20th century, tontines took on a financial character, as in formal savings associations. Every month each member would contribute a fixed share into a "pot." In a 12-member group, each member would receive the pot once a year.

* * * *

The most recent innovation is the interest-bearing tontine. Each month, members bid the amount of interest they will pay for the tontine pot. Interest payments are collected in a separate loan fund and were distributed to members when the tontine is dissolved. Tontines are usually formed for two-year periods and were generally limited to 24 members.

In contrast, banks here pay 7 percent annual interests on savings, and lend money at 13 percent a year. Inflation is about 13 percent. Interest earned on savings is subject to a 10 percent tax, while tontines go unrecorded.

The more advantageous rates offered by tontines can be traced to their lack of overhead, their ability to set rates according to supply and demand and their high payment record.

* * * *

...Tontines, built on trust, are generally made up of homogeneous groups — people from the same ethnic background, the same workplace or the same neighborhood.

"When people go to banks, they don't feel the same urgency to reimburse the loan," Mr Ntsimi said. "If you don't make your payment to the tontine, you are rejected by the community. If you are banned from one group, you are banned from the others." (Emphasis added)

The Koreans use a very similar system. This is from the January 22, 1989 issue of the *Daily News*, titled "Korean Grocers: How They Do It." One quick statement reads:

In many ways, Choi is typical of the 1,400 Korean greengrocers who now own and operate about 90% of the retail fruit-and-vegetable businesses in the five boroughs, according to the Korean Produce Association.

Behind their success are at least three key factors: a willingness to work more hours than most competitors will; reliance on strong *family* and community ties, and money [thank you], because things go faster and cheaper that way.

Families are people who experience a *shared* history, which is the basis for their shared identity. They're not just a bunch of people who happen to live in the same house. What makes them family is not merely being born to the same mother and father, but it is the common experience that they have as a family that ties them together. That commonality of experience and blood is used as a basis for their economic advancement. Strong families, community ties, and cash money...things go faster and cheaper that way.

Read this piece, ladies and gentlemen, if you think you need to go banks to start a business. "When they [the Koreans] needed $60,000 to go in business they raised it in cash." They raised it in cash; not borrowing: Cash among themselves.

"When I have Bronx store, no have money. Everybody help with money. This time, easy to help me; I have credit."

He's not talking about the bank; he's talking about his own people. He built the store. He says he does $10,000 worth of business each week, from which he profits $3,000 to $4,000. That's a tremendous turnover on investment. "Choi doesn't like borrowing from real banks." If you can get $50,000 or $100,000 through friends, that's a *real* bank. But we are made to think it isn't a bank unless it's their [White-folk's] bank.

He [Choi] says, 'That's dangerous. Loan at the bank. If a business falters, the bank will, unlike one's family, insist on prompt repayment no matter what, Choi says.'

In the same paper, another article referred to as "Cultivating Cash," states the following:

"The Korean people have taken over the fruit vegetable business in New York," says Andrew Beltram, a long-time worker at the Hunts Point Terminal Market. "And they can make the fruits and vegetables more beautiful than anybody else. That's for sure. Sometimes you see 20 buyers over there, and 18 of them are Koreans."

Koreans now own about 90% of the fruit-and-vegetable stores in the city and buy 40% of the wholesale produce supply daily at Hunts Point.

That robust growth, says local Korean business leaders, has been accomplished with money raised almost exclusively within the Korean community, usually from personal savings or loans from relatives, friends, and fraternal or business associations.

* * * *

Still another funding source is the money-pooling *keh*, a kind of very informal, unchartered loan club.

Though not illegal, the kehs operate outside U.S. banking laws. For Koreans and other immigrants who find it hard to get banks to take a risk on them the kehs have become an important alternative.

A typical keh consists of 10 to 12 people. Each kicks in the same amount of cash each month to a kitty. Then, on a rotating basis, the entire kitty is loaned to the members, one at a time. Each member, including the borrower, keeps up the monthly payments until each member has gotten a loan at least once. By the time the cycle is complete, each member has borrowed and paid back the whole loan.

The article also talks of how they raise money in the Church and other ways. What is this, ladies and gentlemen? People using History and Tradition.

Our Afrikan-Caribbean brothers and sisters have remembered that tradition. But Afrikan Americans, in an effort to wrongly identify with and imitate White people have forgotten the tradition that could give us the advantage of the very wealth that's right under our feet and in our pockets. Because we have forgotten our history and our tradition and will not identify with it, we can only enrich other people. Then we say,

"History ain't gonna make you money." *No, it's the lack of knowledge of history that doesn't make you money!*

If we get back into our history, get back into our tradition, we'll make money! I'm not an Afrikan who tells us to identify with poverty. I think that the more we identify with our Afrikan tradition the richer we're going to become as people. I'm not here to sell poverty as a virtue. I'm not here to assert that poverty-stricken and welfare-laden people are somehow more virtuous and righteous than people who are making a decent living; that's not my style. We can't say that we are poor and our nations are suffering as a result of our wealth being stolen when if we take that wealth back we won't be richer. How is taking back what belongs to us going to keep us poor? A sure sign, then, of getting back into one's Afrikan self is becoming wealthier, ladies and gentlemen. Does that frighten us? Has the world so convinced us that as a Black people we're destined to be poor? Some of us have that thought and that's why many of us are frightened of money and wealth. That has been inculcated into us by religions and churches, and the very ones inculcating it in us are living quite well.

Amnesia means an undiscovered self, an emptiness, a self incapable of self-understanding, incapable of understanding its own motivations, a self incapable of self-direction and self-determination, a reactionary self, a self that does not understand others or the world in which it exists — a fatalistic externalized self. To rediscover one's history is not only an act of self-discovery; it is an act of self-creation — a resurrection from the dead, a tearing away of the veil, a revelation of the mystery.

To discover our history is to discover our somethingness (beingness) before someone else created us. To come to know ourselves as we were prior to our re-creation by aliens means we will be in charge of our own becoming, the creators of our own consciousness, the creation of ourselves as namers of the world, the namers of ourselves which gives us the power of self determination and self-direction.

What is the past? Where is the past?
  Is it nothing which was something?
Is it something left behind — discarded, detached, forgotten?
  — without influence and therefore of no account?
Does it or can it exist outside the mind and memory of man?
    Or is it not present in our genes where we carry the
      evolutionary existence of our kind?
Are we not then its present unfolding, its evolvement and
    manifestation?
Or is it not congealed in concrete and mortar,
    stone and steel structures and folkways,
      traditions, mores and ways of relating?
Is it not still present in its negation, its
    reconstitution, when it is transformed
      into something new?
Is history ever forgotten, or is it merely transformed?
    Even in the new, history still remains
For the new is fashioned from the old
    Therefore, what is now is fashioned from before
Hence, we never leave history behind
    Isn't the new, then, something old?
History — conscious or unconscious, comprehended or
    uncomprehended — never ceases to be;
      it is only transformed
As transformation, history is always here and now...
    Here today, there tomorrow
History is past, present and future:
    History is destiny
If we *will* to transform destiny we must will to transform
    history!

Response Period

Question: [Unclear]

Brother Wilson: The tradition I mentioned is referred to as tontine in the Cameroon, but I think another West Afrikan word for it is Esusu (coming out of Nigeria). I believe that the word *Susu* still remains in the Caribbean-Afrikan tradition. One of the beautiful things about it is that it can be practiced in families and small groups, between any number of groups. Thus we can plan in this fashion for the raising of money and funding of our economic development. I think this piece I just read about the Korean can also be instructive.

There is a book by Ivan Light called *Ethnic Enterprises in America*, which talks about ethnicity in America in terms of economics. In the main lecture I skipped over a section that dealt with history as *sociotherapy*. We have to use history as a means of reconstituting our personality and restructuring ourselves. If we found these kinds of economic organizations it also becomes necessary to restructure social relations to foster trust, reliability and other positive social characteristics. To go into them purely as economic operations — given the tremendous brainwashing that many of us as Afrikan-Americans have received, and the tremendous amount of alienation that has been projected into our personality — sometimes means that we may set ourselves up for disappointment. So we should plan on a number of levels. One level, of course, is the economic one; the other (which I think is the most fundamentally important one) is developing a strong sense of social belongingness in the group. Getting people to meet their monthly obligation (or however you choose to put money in the pot) pretty much relies on the group's ability to apply social pressure and upon the person's fear of social ostracism and the loss of esteem in that group. If the person does not fear a loss of esteem or does not fear social pressure then you will have people dropping out when they get their "million," leaving you in the lurch. So a part of the deal is we must figure out ways that we can build a very strong social unit.

As a matter of fact, in part of this Cameroonian article, when members got to a situation where they could not meet the obligations of the group...their social ties were so strong that some of them actually committed suicide rather than not meet the obligations to their group. I'm not suggesting that people go that deeply; however, I do want to stress the importance of first rebuilding and overcoming the alienation that has been projected into us as a people. You don't need a wholesale structured organization with this kind of plan; it can begin in the home, the community, within your social group. From there it can again begin to become tradition.

Question: I think of the Church as a very valuable institution. How do you see the Church and what should it become?

Brother Wilson: Of course, the major role of the Church is one of propagating and encouraging spirituality, ethics and rightful behavior among people...some people would say salvation, also. But the Church is a social institution like any other institution; it does not have to be stuck with that definition and perception of itself.

When you look at ads on TV and hear them on the radio you'll note that they are designed to by-pass a person's critical and analytical scrutiny. They're designed to speak directly to the emotions so that the person acts in terms of feelings instead of reason. Therefore, emotions are the bread and butter of advertising and ultimately (in this society) the bread and butter of the economic/social system. So often we, as Afrikans in America, are encouraged to be emotional and spiritual; often we confuse the two things, to the exclusion of critical thinking. We are kept in this "emotional-spiritual state," and it's a bogus kind of state. It opens us to manipulation by external forces such that we cannot bring to bear on our everyday problems common sense and reasoning. So while the Church may see its primary role as maintaining spirituality, fostering an emotional-spiritual relationship with God, it must also recognize that we are a people living on Earth and that we are a people who must feed and protect our children and our economic interests. Therefore, the Church can and should play an economic role in Afrikan American life.

There's an interesting book by R. H. Tawney called *Religion and the Rise of Capitalism*. Also, Weber wrote a book in this vein as well as about the relation of Protestantism and Capitalism, showing that there's a very clear relationship between the founding of Protestantism and the advancement/ development of Western capitalism. Additionally, it shows that there's a relationship between the nature and the theology of the Catholic Church and certain economic structures. So whether you want to recognize it or not, the Church and Religion are intimately related to the economic and social structure. So the Church is not separated from money and economics by any stretch of the imagination. This means that we, as Black people, have the right to redefine the Church in ways that advance our interests, not only economic interests, but social, political, and many other interests in our lives. We need to look at the Church in the context of Afrikan life and see how the Church (without losing its spiritual and ethical mission) can also function to enhance Afrikan economic, social and political life. Often, people who are economically crushed and economically exploited are people who are weighed down with a sense of guilt, sin and other kinds of problems. If we study the theology and the life of Jesus, we will read of his struggle with the ideology coming out of the major religious establishment of his time. That establishment was also a part of an economic order and structure that rationalized and idealized the then economic structure in such a way that people were literally forced into poverty, and in many instances forced into sin and degradation.

The Church, by restructuring itself and by revising its view of itself economically and its role economically, not only can enhance the material well-being of the people, but also can better carry out its spiritual/ethical function as an institution. The Black Church has tremendous value as an economic institution. We have church institutions now creating housing which means that we can begin to use the Church and it can become an instrument for the Black ownership of its communities, lands and properties. These Churches are nationally organized institutions. They have hierarchies and systems of communications, etc. which means that we already have national organizations and national networks in the forms of our church organizations. This means that much more information can be carried through our churches. These churches can build and encourage businesses. If they build businesses across this country we can then build a national network of Black businesses which will lay the foundation for Black manufacturing. It doesn't do us any good to manufacture and have no place to sell our products. But when the Church brings its political weight to bear and demands White and other merchants who own supermarkets and other businesses make room for a Black manufactured products, then Black manufacturers can get on the shelves of these supermarkets, department stores and other kinds of outlets. When the Church creates shopping malls, buildings and other things, it creates jobs for construction. It then stimulates the building, manufacturing and business organizations. So much could grow out of the Church viewing itself as an economic unit.

Once you build this distribution system and it becomes a national system, which means we are organized as a nation (economically), we then are in a position to create a relationship with our Afrikan family overseas. Then, with the power that we and the Church have economically and politically, we can open up the United States (which is one of the largest economic markets in the world) to the sale of Afrikan products. We then can receive those products and be responsible for their distribution in this nation. Thus we can then enrich our Afrikan brothers, laying the basis for their manufacturing and technological development, because they'll have the American markets open to them. What would happen if we sold as many Afrikan-made radios and boom-boxes to Afrika's adolescents as the Japanese are selling? Before long Afrikans would be in a technologically advanced position, rather like that of Japan and the other nations.

So the viewing of the Church and other organizations not only as spiritual organizations but also as economic organizations can lay the foundation and basis for economic/political advancement of Afrikan Man in this world. If we only narrowly see ourselves as a spiritual people — become "other worldly" and only see ourselves as living well after we die — then, of course we're going to catch hell in two places: on Earth and after we die.

Question: I am presently taking a course in Western history. Can you state any suggestions on how I can maneuver in this class as a student?

Brother Wilson: I'm not one who advocates only the taking of Afrikan courses. I believe that if you've really achieved your identity then you can walk among any people; the white mentality is not going to rub off on you. If you know who you are and what you're about you can expose yourself to other people and other people's knowledge. There's nothing wrong with understanding the psychology of other people, and we must understand that psychology by studying the history of their civilizations, etc. The important thing is that we have an Afrikan perspective when we do so.

When you have an Afrikan perspective and consciousness you can take that knowledge and transform it for your own use. Just as the European knowledge of Afrikan history, civilization and culture — and, believe me, they have the knowledge — is used to European advantage, we can use the knowledge of European history and so-called civilization to our own advantage. It's the learning of European history and so-called civilization in the absence of a knowledge of who and what we are that destroys us, not just the learning them or the studying of them. It's the studying of them in the absence of this knowledge, i.e., knowledge of Afrikan history. When you read the history of Shaka Zulu and other Afrikan leaders you will learn political science; you will learn how to control nations and empires; you will learn what destroys nations and what maintains nations and groups; you will learn statecraft and

58

administration. You will learn all of those things because those things are embedded in the history of our people.

So if you have grounded yourself and your personality in your own history, in Afrikan tradition, and your consciousness is Afrocentric, then the European courses can be of value to you. On a certain level you can "enjoy" them. You can enjoy the pleasure of seeing through them. You can enjoy determining why they are distorted. You can see the lies. It really becomes a challenge, a "pleasurable" challenge in a way to see the intellectual shallowness of it all, to see the backwardness of it all, to see the regressiveness contained in it all. Much of European philosophy is regressive and infantile. Afrikan philosophy is exceedingly profound. Just because we don't have Afrikan philosophy written in books doesn't mean it's not profound. There's profound philosophy, ideology and outlook in Afrikan tradition.

The beauty of Afrikan tradition is that it is not alienated in a book; it is part and parcel of the total Afrikan personality. Studying European disciplines under those circumstances can be of supreme value. With an Afrikan-centered consciousness we can take from that tradition that which is of value to us, that which we can use, and also have a basis for rejecting that which is of little or no value or which is harmful and dangerous. Under those circumstances it is no problem to deal with it, per se. That's why I recommend to Afrikans in universities that they get a solid grounding in Afrikan history/tradition *before* they take the other courses. Then, move on to the other courses, study them fully and transform them in your interest.

Culture and tradition are intellectual tools. When we rediscover our culture and tradition, when Afrikan culture and tradition becomes a part of us, we are going to have an intellectual explosion such as this world has never before witnessed. When we rediscover ourselves, our creativity is released. One of the reasons European history is written the way it is, is to restrict our creativity to music, dance, games, and things that do not directly challenge Europeans. When we re-internalize our culture we're going to gain our genius again; we will regain our analytical skills and use them in our interest. Because once we know Afrikan philosophy we have a basis upon which we can critically analyze other philosophies; we have a basis on which we can evaluate what other people say; we have a basis for measuring what other people are saying and doing. If we do not have that, a part of our intellect is lost and we'll find ourselves studying one European's criticism of the other European. We have Afrikans today quoting one European as against another, when you should be saying, "A pox on both your houses; I have a whole different perspective, both of you are wrong." This is real.

When we examine the world today, the wars in so-called Third World countries, look and see if they're not fighting each other over European ideologies, instead of basing their political ideology (rationalizations) upon a profound analysis of their own history and experience and developing what their economic/political/social program should be based on an analysis of themselves (thereby developing their own intellectual tools as they do so). Instead they grasp on to an imported, foreign ideology; one getting it from the United States, the other one getting it from Russia — and they kill each other over them.

The acquiring of an Afrikan-centered ideology, the infusion of an ideology developed out of one's own history and experience, reduces civil war, mutual destruction and the kinds of troubles we see our people in so much today. Lenin said something like "the Capitalist will sell you the rope by which to hang him." The European by exposing his history, ideology and knowledge the way he does is literally putting the rope in our hands with which we can hang him. But we can't hang him unless we possess an Afrikan-centered consciousness. So get it — go into the courses and get the rope!

Endnotes

a. This section was excerpted from a presentation done on February 15, 1991, under the title *Moving Beyond White Racism and Civil Rights to Afrikan Revolution.* We determine this piece to have defined, corroborated, and complemented the preceding discussion on the period of Reconstruction.

b. Jackson, John G. (1987) *Black Reconstruction in South Carolina.* Dallas, Texas: American Atheist Press.

c. See *The City Sun,* November 21-27, 1990, "The Death of a Black-owned Bank" by Clinton Cox. This bore out the Wilson statement made *years* prior to the actual happening, the demise of Freedom National Bank in Harlem, New York.

Bibliography

Bennett, L. (1967) *Black Power U.S.A.: The Human Side of Reconstruction, 1867-1877.* Chicago, IL: Johnson Publications.

Kovel, Joel (1970) *White Racism: A Psychohistory* N.Y.: Columbia University Press.

Light, Ivan (1972) *Ethnic Enterprises in America: Business and Welfare Among Chinese, Japanese and Blacks.* Los Angeles: University of California.

Tawney, Richard H. (1926) *Religion and the Rise of Capitalism.* Peter Smith.

Weber, Max (1958) *The Protestant Ethic and the Spirit of Capitalism,* New York: Charles Scribner's sons.

Part Two

EUROCENTRIC
POLITICAL DOGMATISM

*Its Relationship to the Mental
Health Diagnosis of Afrikan People*

II

A MAJOR DEPARTURE OF BLACK PSYCHOLOGY from Eurocentric psychology or White psychology is the fact that Black psychology is openly and consciously political, and recognizes that the very basis for what we might call mental problems, or other kinds of problems in the Black community, is the political structure, the Eurocentric structure that is present in America, and present in the world.

Eurocentric psychology, while offering us some information of value, is somewhat limited in the fact it generally starts from the standpoint of the so-called family, and sees the family as the cause of mental illness, juvenile delinquency, educational problems, and so forth. It examines the mother-child relationship as the basis for the personality orientation of the patient. However, we must recognize, as Afrikan people, that this approach is inadequate: primarily because it appears to be relatively non-political.

The Politicoeconomic Necessity of Madness

While mental problems, juvenile delinquency and other problems may flow from family relations, we must recognize that relations existing within a family structure are themselves shaped by the political situation in which they are embedded. The relationship between the Black mother and child, the Black father and child, the politics that go on within the Black family structure, the politics of color, the politics of quality of hair, the politics of sexuality and so forth that exist within the Black family, reflect to a very great extent the politics of the larger White-dominated society in which the Black community finds itself. If an effort is made to get at the roots of mental problems and other kinds of problems that exist within the Afrikan

American individual and community, it must begin with an analysis of the political context in which they co-exist.

It must start with the recognition of the fact that juvenile delinquency, criminality, mental problems, family problems, and other kinds of problems which are prevalent in our community, are social necessities, are political necessities. We have stated before, that in order for us as a people to be in the situation we are in, and not be in concentration camps and not have guns pointed at our heads throughout the day, we must be maintained in a particular state of mind. In a sense then, we literally must be out of our minds — and we must be kept out of our minds.

Mental maladaptiveness among our people is a political, social necessity, and therefore is instigated by political, social forces; and a Black psychology must begin with this very fact. This political necessity is in part based on the demographic fact that the European is approximately ten percent (10%) of the world's population. The European inhabits only a small part of this globe. The parts of the globe that the European occupies are relatively resourceless when compared to those occupied by non-European people. And yet, the European is saddled with great wealth, economic and political power. He controls the globe and maintains the world in a state of terror, and has the earth now on the brink of suicide.

We must question how is it that a minority people, a very small percentage of mankind, a people who are essentially resourceless in terms of their natural resources, maintain the power they have. Why is it that the peoples whose lands contain the wealth of the earth are the poorest people? Why is it that Afrika with some twenty (20) or thirty (30) strategic metals that make the space age possible — why is it that the image of Afrika is projected at us time and time again as that of starving children, as societies in disorder, as societies on the verge of disaster? This implies, to my mind, that there must exist a political, social situation wherein the mental orientation of our people must be so structured that the power and the ability of the Europeans to rule this earth are continually maintained.

To a good extent, people are kept out of their minds by means of *contradictions* and *conflicts*: where the mind is faced with what appears to be unresolvable problems and dilemmas and seeks often to escape those contradictions either through the creation of illness, misbehavior, or often through grabbing on to one of the horns of the dilemma — extreme conformity, or through extreme rebellion — all of which are designed ultimately to maintain the status quo. For the European to rule the world as he does today, or at least to intimidate it as he does, contradictions must be a chronic part of the lives of the non-European people...as well as that of the European. The imperialistic European must essentially function in a very devilish fashion. That is, in a fashion that uses *deception* as its major characteristic. Consequently, fundamental values and ways of seeing reality must be reversed. The good must appear to be the bad, the light dark. Truth must be taken for the lie; the lie for truth. Otherwise a small group, such as European people, could not continue to keep the rest of the world out of its mind.

The European hegemonic establishment must project false and injurious ideologies that are accepted by its victims. It must project self-serving ideologies that are seen as givens, as natural. It must project fraudulent ideologies that are seen as not subject to question. When the victims of European imperialistic domination accept its ideologies uncritically, they then accept the rulership and dominance of the imperialistic European. They then begin to identify with the very group that is responsible for their problems.

Individualism and Self-Blame

One of the ideologies (there are a number, but we will look at just one today) projected to maintain European dominance, is the ideology of *individualism*. We hear a great deal today of the *do-your-own-thing* and *I-do-mine* kind of situation; the so-called individualization of success and failure. That is, where individual failure is seen as the result of what we call *personal ineptness* or misbehavior; as a sign of moral inferiority. That is, those peoples and individuals who fail in society fail as a result of problems within themselves, some individual short-coming or ineptness: ultimately, failing as a result of some moral problem within their personalities.

William Graham Sumner, a pioneering and influential American sociologist, indicated that the poor are shiftless and impudent. They are negligent, impractical, and inefficient. That they are the idle and the intemperate, the extravagant and the vicious. Even those people who founded social work and the so-called helping-professions, and who saw themselves as liberals, often saw the behavior and the failure of the victims of Eurocentric domination as a result of their personal misbe-havior or the result of their moral weaknesses. We call this kind of approach the *individual moral sensibility*,[2] which is used to justify the culture of inequality.

That is, this individualism, this *individual moral sensibility* tries to persuade us that this society is equal, and that this society makes available to all individuals equal the opportuni-ties to advance in it, and if they fail, it is the result of their own personal problems. Of course, it becomes obvious that this kind of approach is a rationale and a rationalization by means of which the society itself ignores its own input as far as the failure of a person or people, such as our people, are concerned. It helps us to ignore the impact of the social structure upon individual achievement and mobility. It tends almost literally to try and eradicate the idea that the individual succeeds or fails *within* a social structure.

Since the individual does not succeed or fail in a vacuum but succeeds or fails in a social system, the social system must be taken into consideration when we evaluate individual success and failure. This implies the possibility that the social structure itself may be principally responsible for the success of some and the failure of others. However, a society developed by the

---

[2] This term was borrowed from Michael Lewis' *The Culture of Inequality*. N.Y.: New American Library. 1978.

imperialistic European, who arrogates to himself the dominance and rule over the vast majority of people, cannot afford to truthfully and honestly look at the possibility that it is the structure of the Eurocentric society itself which greatly influences the individual and group fates of our peoples.

While many of our liberal friends may not see the so-called success or failure, or the condition of our people as a result of a moral problem, and they would possibly argue that the poor are no more morally decrepit than are the middle-class or are the upper-class, they still tend to maintain the social status quo in a modified form by projecting a kind of scientistic ideology, one that appears at first to be neutral in its orientation.

This ideology speaks of such apparently neutral things such as the psycho-dynamic make-up of the individual; it speaks of weak egos; lack of personal integration; conflicts between id, ego, and super ego; the dark side of the personality overtaking the light side of the personality. All kinds of systems, names and intra-psychic mechanisms are invoked to explain the subjugation of some people and the domination of others, the so-called success of some and the failure of others.

We hear sociologists talk about cultural commitments, i.e., those who are committed to mainstream values and mainstream behavior as against those who belong to an ostensible culture of poverty, who have absorbed a different system of values. They offer us family background, and they offer us various types of child-rearing approaches that presumably do or do not prepare the individual to deal with middle-class White society; family backgrounds and approaches which do or do not provide the individual with the ability to solve his or her social problems. Educationists go deeply into the cognitive structures of the victims and indicate the means by which they are deficient in academic or other abilities. Social psychologists offer us explanations in terms of interpersonal competence and behavior, and the failure of communications to occur between family members and other people. We get a host of definitions and a host of "explanations." However, we rarely, if ever, get an approach that looks at the political system and the political aims of the imperialistic European, and in what ways those aims contribute to the critical situation that we see ourselves in today.

American social scientists, especially psychologists and sociologists and the so-called helping-professionals, come to the aid of European domination with what we call *deficiency explanations*. We note that in the study of the Black child, and in the study of Black people within our universities, we get a bevy of deficiency terminologies or jargon and we get long semesters of courses about the *deviant behavior* of Black people. We get courses that use the White middle-class child or the White middle-class itself as a measure for all other peoples, and those individuals and people who do not measure up to their standards are seen as deviant or deficient in one form or another.

Insanity as a Model of Sanity

The most insane people on the earth today are used as models for sanity. The sanity of the racist European itself is not questioned. The insanity of European normality is not questioned. The possibility that what we call *normal* is itself *insane* is not questioned; that the organization of this society, the nature of its human relations, the structure of its economic systems, the values that motivate it, are the result of the madness of a people.

Have we ever taken time to step back and step out of our "normal" minds for a minute, and look at the madness that exists around us? Have we ever stopped for a moment and noted the madness that motivates us to jam into these subways every morning; that motivates us to work endlessly and compulsively; that motivates us to feel guilty in a moment of leisure; that motivates us to consume endlessly; that motivates us to be the victims of all kinds of erratic fashions? Have we seen the craziness that peers out at us from our television screens? Have we recognized that the television screen projects little reality at all? That we measure ourselves against what we look at there! That TV advertising is designed to keep us in a state of frustration and dissatisfaction, and designed to inculcate in us a sense of inferiority, and designed to keep us from facing reality and confronting the truth, to divert us from the pitifulness of our situation!; to not let us recognize as a people that we are in a precarious situation, and that our very biological survival is in question. We sit in front of the TV set and look at those little families whose members who are so polite to each other, who are so witty, who wait for each other to get through speaking before speaking themselves, who lay in just the right line just at the right time, and who resolve their problems so neatly and beautifully, and assume that they represent the typical family.

What would happen if we really saw it like it *is* on TV? You know, families where people really go "up-side" each other's heads, cut each other off. If reality was projected there, rather than the pretense, the fantasies, and the fairy tales that are placed there so that we as Black people imagine that what we see as White families on television really exists, and are left with an inferiority complex, asking, "Why can't our families get along like that, be sweet to each other like that, be concerned with each other like that?"

We must look at the psychopathology of everyday life and must recognize we cannot have it both ways. We cannot talk about a people who have enslaved us, who discriminate against us, who insult us, who do all manner of other things against us, and then use them as models of normality. We cannot use these people who are criminals, who have the world on the edge of suicide, who are now getting ready to negotiate about how many bombs they are going to keep for destroying the earth — how they are going to distribute death to the rest of the world — as models for normality!

These people, the Khrushchevs, Chernenkos, Breshnevs, the killers of many hundreds of thousands of people — Study them! Study the hierarchy of the Russian Empire that rules over Poland and Yugoslavia and the nations of Eastern Europe. I don't give a hoot whether they are Marxist, or Leninists, or anything else, but I know what they are as human beings. And we know the behavior that they have exhibited in the name of their political philosophies. We know that imperialist Europeans stole nations and destroyed hundreds of thousands of Amerindians, Afrikans and other peoples; and whose every step in other people's nations has done little but destroy the local people, drive them out of their minds, destroy their cultures and rob them of their wealth. And yet, these people are held up as normal, and are used as the standard against which we measure ourselves as a people, and are used as models for us to determine the way we wish our children to behave.

History, Psychology and Ideology

If we look at the history of the European imperialists we see their psychology. As I have said on numerous occasions, the psychology of the rulers of this world, the psychology of eurocentrically oriented people is not in the psychology books, but in the *history* books; and one merely needs then to read their history to get at their psychology. And that history, of course, is not written by me, not written by Black scholars. It is not written by us "prejudiced nationalists." It is written, of course, by the imperialists themselves, and therefore is a form of self-indictment, and it is there for all to see. It is an admission in and of itself of the insane nature of the people who are in the control of the world today. We must then recognize that given this history and the desire on the part of the hegemonic European to maintain the status quo, the ideologies and other institutions created by them are created and maintained as a means of supporting the status quo itself.

If we look at European imperialistic history and find that history embarrassing and hurtful, then we are compelled to look at the ideologies that have flowed from that history. We cannot look and shake our heads in sadness at the enslavement of our people, the death and killing of the Amerindians, the creation of the holocaustic weapons, the wars that have been perpetrated by an imperialistic people, and split that kind of information off from the ideologies put forth by those people.

They áre one and the same, and are part and parcel of the same reality. And it is this attempt on our part and this attempt by the system to segment and cut off these things one from the other, to compartmentalize life, and to compartmentalize reality, that to a great extent forms the basis for our mental, physical, and other kinds of problems that are existent in our community today.

This system is one then that on one hand teases and provokes, and on the other hand denies. Its individualistic sensibility encourages us to dream big dreams, to imagine that the best of everything is within our grasp and within our reach, and at the same time it denies the possibilities for these dreams to become reality. It tells our young teenagers that if they do not wear the right kinds of sneakers, and the right kinds of jeans, and possess the right kinds of eye-glass frames on their faces, that they are nothing. It tells them that if they have not achieved along the lines of the society dictates, that they are worthless, and at the same time denies them the opportunity and the structure, the means by which the achievements can be attained. And therefore, our teenagers and we as adults are caught in a major contradiction, in a major dilemma. And when we fail to deal with it we are told that it is the result of some deficiency in our personality, some genetic problem, some sub-cultural problem.

This kind of ideology, of course, not only is an ideology that rationalizes the status quo, and removes the responsibility from the social structures developed by Europeans, and removes the responsibility from that structure for bringing about the conditions inherent in the community and in individuals. It is also designed to drive us insane. So this ideology is not merely a means of rationalizing the status quo, but is also a projective means of creating an abnormal state of mind. Because when the individual is provoked to strive and then has his legs "broken" at the same time and is told that it is his fault, the individual's self-respect is threatened. The individual's identity is destroyed. The individual's self-concept and self-esteem are washed out. Once the victim accepts the ideology of individualism, he is then set (when he fails to make it within the system) to blame himself in a very destructive sort of way; to begin to question his or her competence, to doubt his or her ability, to doubt his or her worth and ultimately, to hate himself.

But self-hatred is not only an individual reaction. It becomes part of a social system, because the individual who hates himself hates other people who remind him of himself. And therefore, when he looks out at his sisters and brothers he also looks at himself; and if he questions the adequacy and competence of himself, he questions the adequacy and competence of his sisters and brothers. So then, the experience of failure and the experience of not achieving in society not only becomes an individual experience; it becomes a social experience and a social disease. Therefore, the philosophy and the ideology of individualism is not an ideology that attacks the individual: It is an ideology that attacks the whole of a community. It is a part of a community ideology designed to maintain the dominance of one community over another; to maintain the dominance of the Eurocentric community over the Afrikan community.

The individual who accepts the ideology of *individualism*, and sees his failure to achieve as the result of some deficiency in his personality, and thinks that opportunities exist and that if he merely had the right personality he could make the best of these opportunities, when the achievement does not occur, is faced with a major contradiction. He is faced with what we call a *sense of cognitive dissonance*. That certain things do not jibe. Dissonance, contradictions and conflicts are painful and are hard to bear. They make life discomforting, and hence motivate the individual to seek to resolve the contradictions — to try and remove these contradictions and to put them out of existence.

Coping with Contradictions

There are a number of means by which we seek to resolve certain contradictions in our lives. We may excuse them by saying that the circumstances which have determined our lives, particularly the failures in our lives, are beyond our control. That it is other peoples who are totally responsible for the situation that we are in, and therefore we have no control over it.

While this to a degree is true, it also can lead to some other psychological problems in the individual. It can lead to the possibility that the individual becomes apathetic; gives up and resigns from life, gives up trying and begins to believe that he or she is powerless. Unfortunately, the resignation and the apathy of too many of our people are part of the means by which the system maintains itself. The fear of trusting and uniting with each other, the fear of coming together and solving our problems together, the belief that it is just not in us to unite and solve our problems and overcome the dominance of European imperialism itself becomes a part of the problem and helps to maintain the system. Others try to deal with the discrepancy between what the system says they can achieve and our failure to achieve by lowering their personal aspirations, by, in a sense, fitting into a lesser place that the society reserves for them. Others try to inflate their achievements, to inflate their personalities.

We see many of us along the highways and byways being very boastful, being very egocentric, bragging a great deal, pumping ourselves up, pumping even small achievements up into giant achievements. We see it even infecting the Black Nationalist community that buries itself in the great history of Egypt and the great empires of Afrika. Yes, I am speaking of the kind of historicism that has developed in this community as a means of not confronting reality! Of people who live their lives in history, and dig among the pyramids of Egypt, and dig among the lost kingdoms of Mali and Songhai, and who build themselves a false pride, and pump themselves up about the achievements of our history — without facing the perils of current reality and preparing themselves for the future. The Black Nationalist who makes us feel good — and pumps us up; and makes us gloat and glow about our great past, and does not deal with the present; and does not educate in terms of coping with the future; and does not adequately prepare us to remove the European from power, to remove these insane people who are about to destroy the earth and life itself — is functioning in the interest of the status quo. And those people who holler about the devilishness of the White man, the evilness of the White man, and leave it at that, still are not necessarily performing a full service for our people. There must be other things involved. We see then, many individuals blowing up their minor accomplishments as a means of ignoring the realities of their situation.

If accepting the truth about the situation of Afrikan peoples and other people in the world today means exposing the European to himself, of course he is going to ignore that exposé. I was on a radio program one night, and a lady told of how her child was left in tears because of a lesson that her White teacher was giving in "slave history." What's amazing is that they can teach such history to our people. But the problem was that the child left with a greater sense of frustration and inferiority. The parent was questioning me to a degree as to whether (or at least it was implied) slave history should be taught since may it upset some of our children.

For many White teachers to teach Black history in its objective and correct form would be to condemn the very people who are in control of the society itself. It would mean that the teacher, the White teacher who teaches it, will condemn herself or himself. And it also means that, often, even those of us who are Black, when we do not teach our history correctly, would point to our own collusion with the system. This often occurs because what is discussed is the nature of slavery and the conditions of slavery, but not the nature and condition of the slave-master. And the questions that are dealt with are not questions concerning the mental stability and characteristics of those who enslaved us, and the question is not the fact that these people are still influential today, and the question as to whether they should continue to be influential is not dealt with at all.

So consequently, our children are left with an inferiority complex, the subject is left half unexplored, and even its being brought up and taught serves as a means of maintaining the system while appearing to be a liberal concession to the radicals of the sixties (1960s).

We must recognize that many Americans have a stake in ensuring the continuation of the failure of large segments of its population — particularly of the Afrikan American population. We must recognize that contradiction in this society is of major importance in determining the problems of our communities. That it is the people without love who talk about love most often. It is the people who are ready to go to war, and have gone to war and destroyed hundreds and thousands, who talk about peace. It is the people who destroy our children's minds in schools who talk a great deal about education. And we will see these kinds of contradictions going on and on repeatedly. We will see even in the very legal structure of the system its contradictions which conspire to destroy those who are not a part of the ruling class or group.

Procedural Liberties, Personal Restraints

The constitution of the United States, as beautiful as it may sound, is ultimately an elitist document. The Russian constitution is a most beautiful document, when you read it. And yet we see a minority of White Russians ruling over Moslems, other minorities, and other Europeans, despite what the constitution says.

The constitution of our nation guarantees what we call *procedural liberties*, while not guaranteeing what we may call the real nitty-gritty substantial liberties. What do we mean by that? It guarantees that certain procedures will be followed; that we can go to court, that we will be heard before a so-called jury of our peers and so forth. But does it guarantee a freedom from hunger? Does it guarantee housing, health care, and true education? Does it guarantee full employment? Does it guarantee safe working conditions? Does it guarantee a non-polluted Earth? Does it guarantee true equality and equal distribution of resources? The constitution does not guarantee those things. It guarantees us certain procedural rights and rules. It says, then, that we can go to court the same way the

77

rich people go to court. That we can be heard in a court of law, that we must be read our *Miranda rights* upon arrest.

But there is a difference between procedure and what actually happens. Certainly we may be read our rights, and certainly we may go to court — but without the money to pay for a good lawyer? Belonging to the wrong ethnic group, belonging to wrong class — while we may go through procedure — does not guarantee justice. Consequently, the justice and legal establishments become the very sources of injustice and illegality. We are therein faced with a contradiction wherein the very law and order that is written into the constitution becomes a doublestandard. I remember reading a phrase once that said, "the freedom of the press belongs to those who own the press." We can thus reiterate that the constitution and the legal system in this society are not a neutral instrument, and that the law belongs to those who write it, and to those who use it to control the resources of a society.

Business crime is more damaging than most working-class crime and so-called lower-class crime. As a matter of fact, we tend not to even see business-crime as crime itself, but instead as violations of codes, as not following procedure, even though it may rob people of jobs. It may rob people of their very lives. How many people from DuPont will be arrested and put in jail and locked away for killing those thousands of Indians?[3] How many people will be destroyed or executed as the result of the stealing of monies, of millions and millions of dollars from the general populace as a whole? Will Chase Manhattan be permitted to go out of business? Or will Citibank, for the mistake of making bad loans? No, they won't. What will happen? They will rob the very monies out of our pockets so that they may stay in business.

It has been established that while robbery, burglary, auto theft, and larceny account for 15 percent of theft against property, embezzlement, fraud, forgery, and commercial theft

---

[3] USA's transnational corporation Union Carbide pesticide gas explosion on December 3, 1984, in Bhopal, India, resulted in at least 2,000 deaths.

(the so-called white-collar crimes) are responsible for 78 percent of crimes against property. It is difficult for people to even see a so-called top business executive as a criminal. The very concept of criminal has an image attached to it. We shall find, of course, that to a great extent that image is non-European, non-middle-class and non-upper-class, but is an image that portrays the so-called lower-classes (or non-Europeans). It is of interest to note that Zacarro, husband of the vice presidential candidate [Geraldine Ferraro], could steal millions and pay a thousand-dollar ($1,000) fine — and continue in business — while our sons and daughters who may steal nickels are sent to jail, and executed, done in, beaten, and assassinated by the police. We are gouged for rent and other kinds of things by the system; yet those that gouge us are perceived as pillars of the community.

These are the kinds of contradictions that breed disrespect for the law, and disrespect for those who enforce the law. It does not matter if a law is written in neutral terms. What really matters is whether that law is enforced non-discriminately; and this society is one that is famous for writing beautiful laws, which are enforced in a non-equal fashion. We recognize that the policeman is not merely an officer of the law, not merely there to enforce the law, but that the policeman has discretion in enforcing the law, and can determine when and under what circumstances (to a good extent) the law will be enforced, and against what people, regardless of how that law is written.

So a law that may be on the books in a non-discriminatory manner, can be executed in a very discriminatory fashion. Therefore, we recognize that the Black individual who exhibits the same so-called behavior (that is designated as criminal by a cop) as a White individual, is far more likely to be arrested, convicted, and jailed for that behavior. So a cop makes a determination based on the individual's race, upon the individual's sexuality, upon the individual's political and class characteristics, as to whether arrest, conviction, and so forth will take place.

So we recognize that a law, even though it is written in neutral terms, may be used for the purpose of intimidation, harassment, and a means of immobilizing individuals. The very charges against arrested individuals may depend upon the racial nature, the class, and the politics of the individual's background. These are the kinds of contradictions that have destroyed the personalities of our people, that have destroyed our self-confidence, have destroyed our self-concept as a people.

These contradictions, therefore, have created a psychic situation that is often diagnosed as neurosis and psychosis; that are often used as a means of maintaining a political system as such. We are talking about the *New York Eight*[a] here. We see again a system of law that is being used to enforce thought-control; of people being arrested for so-called conspiracy for what they may or may not think. We see a system of law enforcement that spent great time and energy, that went on for almost two years of eavesdropping into people's personal lives, of placing electronic bugs all over the households of these people, of putting eavesdropping equipment in every room (including the bathroom), that puts bugging equipment into their telephones, that picked up the conversations of not only of those individuals who were supposedly involved in the conspiracy but those other individuals who may have called and talked to them for various other reasons. We see a system that generates a law that says — you can now detain people without bail if they are perceived as some kind of major danger to the community — that soon after it passes that law goes right out and arrests a group of people and comes prepared to destroy those people.

We see a system that is not so much concerned with defending the individual as defending the prerogatives of the state and making certain that the state has a monopoly on the weapons, that the citizens are disarmed, not so much as a means of preventing citizens from killing each other — but as a means of keeping the citizens from killing the government that rules over them!

We must be aware of the European who discusses a lot of social issues in terms of individual-behavior such as, 'we don't want people out there taking the law in their own hands.' It is the police that take the law into their own hands, when the police engage in racial discrimination, when a policeman beats, shoots, destroys and kills our people in the streets. It is the police who are taking the law into their own hands — not the people themselves. It is the police who are the vigilantes for the establishment, and for maintaining the status quo. The situation is reversed. It is the police, then, who have the means of holding people hostage in jails and in prisons; and who harass our people; and who lock our people in dungeons; and who exercise penalties and terror. *Who is going to guard the guardians of our so-called law?*

We see the law, then, may not be the problem; it is the execution of the law. We see the law used as the means of repression of dissent. The police are used as the means of maintaining the social status quo and social order, not so much when a person is purportedly disturbing-the-peace, but where a person threatens to disturb the social system itself. Police officers often see Americanism as being equivalent to capitalism; that one cannot be American if one is not also capitalist. And therefore to be anti-capitalist is to be anti-American. To be for a different system of distributing the wealth of the nation, which belongs to the nation, is to be anti-American. To concern oneself with a more equitable means of distributing justice and freedom, to question the current system of inequality, is to be perceived as un-American and a *threat-to-national-security*; it is to be made fair game for repression and the denial of the democratic rights that are supposedly guaranteed by the Constitution. We see that often the only crime of many people, such as *the Eight*, is to think in different terms and to talk about a different type of arrangement of social relations. But that speech and that thought laid the basis for their very rights being taken away from them — the right of bail and other rights.

Under the guise of defending democracy, the security agencies of our national legal departments are able to deny so-called dissenters their democratic rights, and to move the nation closer to a police-state; which is exactly what we are seeing here. And therefore we see telephones tapped, offices raided, records and funds of dissident organizations stolen by the police themselves. We see agencies of our law enforcement departments engaged in theft, breaking and entering. We see agencies of *the law* engaged in threatening the members of non-conforming groups, maligning the reputation of those who dare to question the system; beating, murdering, arresting and "trumping-up" charges against those who dare even think out loud or indicate that they are looking at other possibilities for dealing with the tremendous problems we have today.

We see a system that uses its procedural rights — rights to a trial, the rights to a jury, the rights to go before a grand jury — as means of repression. Oh, *the Eight* may win their case: But will they really win their case? Did Angela Davis really win her case? Or was the very process of fighting the charges — the years of energy, blood, sweat and tears, the years and the money that went into the defense of Angela and others like her — the very means of repression expressing itself in the system. By the time these individuals get through fighting in the courts that allow them to be heard before "a jury of their peers," the issues and troubles over which they were arrested in the first place often have left them behind or have been destroyed by the very process itself. Their very arrest and their very going through the procedure, even if the procedure is neutral and equal, still intimidates the rest of us, and makes the rest of us conform.

So, we have a system that may even "free" us and then congratulates itself: "Oh, the system works, doesn't it?" But only after a course, it works. But it is set up such that in the end it will still attain its oppressive goals. You have the right to equal housing; the law says so. We even have agencies that we can complain to about being discriminated against. All of that is set up. We have a right to move into any neighborhood we want to — if we can afford it. Here is the system that grants these rights and simultaneously takes away the very means of fully exercising them.

This is a system that uses all types of psycho-controls for law and order. Once we are arrested, once we are convicted, our rights are denied; now we can be subject to electro-shock, psycho-surgery, etc. Recall that in the sixties' (1960s) the dissidents — those who were part of riot situations, those who protested against the oppression of Black people — were seen as sick, were seen as having a problem. And one of the means proposed for dealing with the problem was to cut parts of their brains out; was to go directly into their skulls and lobotomize them, because of a diagnosis of illness, and more than anything else, because of a political diagnosis. Some of you saw the *Amsterdam News*, I believe. It came out Thursday. It discusses the experimentation on our people by the Federal Bureau of Investigation (FBI), Central Intelligence Agency (CIA), and other agencies inside and outside of this country. Even in South Afrika and other places the experimentation on our people is taking place currently — and certainly has taken place in the past. We must recognize that this kind of thing continues and is a part of the so-called *law and order* system that exists today.

Compensation

So these are the contradictions in the system; educational systems that make us dumb, that teach us how not to think; welfare systems that keep us poor; foreign aid that keep our Afrikan nations in states of poverty; religious establishments which are going to send us all to hell; an egalitarian constitution that maintains inequality. It is this system that is projected into and interpreted in the minds of Black parents and Black people, that is also projected into the socioeconomic structure and thereby creates attitudes, negative self-perceptions and frustrations. It is a kind of system that breeds mental problems, problems of criminality, and other kinds of problems that are duly diagnosed by psychologists and sociologists and social workers; that are duly treated by those who are helping-professionals, who ultimately end up helping themselves to us, rather than helping us. As a matter of fact, we could see those professions as a part of the system itself.

Our responses to these contradictions include problems with identity. Some of us respond through over-compensation; those of us who are going to prove to the White-folk that we are the greatest in the world. We see some people succeed as a result of failing; the success is often based on failure; success can be a type of failure. That is one reason why often success does not bring the kind of personal satisfaction and peace that many people seek. And why often the individual, despite all of the material evidences of having succeeded, still feels psychologically cheated — because one can achieve for the wrong reason. So when we achieve to prove to somebody else, to show the White-folk that we can do it as good as they do it, it is a success that still is guaranteed to make us sick. It is motivated by the wrong reason. We must get caught up in succeeding as a total way of life; we then must get caught up in fearing failure; and therefore become obsessive and compulsive. We must have a feeling of pressure, a feeling that imminent disaster is pursuing us at all times. Therefore success becomes a burden, and often we have to drink, smoke and do all other unhealthy kinds of things in order to contend with it. We have the successful people "coking" just as much as the unsuccessful. Because often they have succeeded and failed for the very same reasons; and their very success and failure helps to maintain the status quo.

Are we studying Egyptology to prove to the White man how great we were? And hope one day that when he acknowledges that Egyptians were Afrikans, that he will accept us as human beings? Is our study of Egyptology a personal and collective defense mechanism, a means of dealing with our hurt pride? As a means of trying to slip into the acceptance of White people by the back door? Is our hang-up with history and the exaggeration of certain of our achievements means by which we try to salvage a damaged ego? There is the ache of inferiority that never goes away. And we study, and we study, and we read, and we read, and we learn the hieroglyphics, and we still feel inferior — because we are pushed by the wrong reasons. And when we are motivated by the wrong reasons, even though we may replace the people who rule over us, we will end up being just *like* them.

Our succeeding for the wrong reasons sets our mind up for being inculcated and possessed by the very devil we fight against. And therefore, another revolution will have to be fought, and it will have to be fought against *us*.

Consequently, it is not enough to succeed in the society or to fail. Some people succeed at failing; the White man tells us we're no good and we work very hard showing him he's right. Yes, we find the parallel situation in many parent-child situations. "You will never be nothing," and the child shows them with a vengeance how it will be nothing. "I am going to make you see, mama, every day that I'm nothing. I am going to flaunt my nothing-ness in your face. I am going to make you cry every night, and I'm going to make you go the jail and try to get me out"; because you told me I was just like my daddy — no good, going nowhere. Or else you will do it the other way. "I am going to show you how good I am." And he succeeds, but he succeeds with an emptiness in his heart and in his mind. *Our victory leaves the taste of ashes in our mouths*. We wonder where the happiness went, and we say: "Is this all there is to it?" Nothing hurts like failing, unless it is success. Many of us found out when we broke into White mid-stream America that there is just as much hell in there as it was where we were to begin with.

We have to recognize then that it is not a matter of making it in the system, but a matter of questioning the system itself. It is not just a matter of equality within the system but the very critical looking at the system in and of itself. So many of us in responding to the contradictions projected by this system react with rage, apathy, stereotypy, paranoia, suspiciousness and depression, and mania — and even bourgeois nationalism. Oh, yes, we have some bourgeois nationalist here! It is not only the ruling-class Whites that seek to perceive the condition of our people as a result of the moral failings of our people, or of some moral deficiency. We have to be careful and make sure that we also as a people do not see ourselves that way. Yes, and we as Black Nationalists — well-fed, with jobs — have to be very careful when we think the only thing our less fortunate brothers need is a lesson in Egyptian history, and a lesson in

Black history, and a lesson in morality; and *voila!* when all the Black people find out that they were great Egyptians and great Ghanaians, oh, what a great dream will have come true! Then we will find out that we will be pretty much in the same condition we were in before. What we are fighting against, as Paul said in the Bible, are "principalities, against powers, against the rulers of the darkness of this world, against spiritual wickedness in high places"[4], against a *real "power"*; not just a mind-set, but against real flesh and blood people who are in control of the world's economic system, and social system, and military system. Mere knowledge, morality, values, though of great importance are not going to be enough to extricate us from the situation that we are in.

The Politics of Diagnosis

We are talking about diagnosis and the relationship of mental health diagnosis to political and racial dogmatism. When social workers and psychologists do not begin with the political system, they become obsessed with *diagnostic procedures.* Psychology concerns itself with predicting behavior, with being able to determine to a very fine extent the characteristics and the symptomatologies of various mental illnesses. Mental health disciplines concern themselves with the categorization of behavior and the means by which this process is carried out. Getting obsessively involved with diagnostic procedures, psychologists and others in this area can deceive themselves into thinking they are doing great scientific work, and that they are politically neutral in their approach to life.

Mental problems not only denote a disturbed psyche, that an individual is disturbed, but that that individual disturbs our psyche. When we say an individual is disturbed, we not only indicate that the individual may have problems, but we indicate that we are having problems with the individual. That the individual is not only disturbed, but the individual disturbs

---

[4] Ephesians 6.12.

us. So then, diagnosis involves a dualistic relationship, not only in terms of what behavior is exhibited by the patient but how that behavior reflects upon others and the person who is making the diagnosis itself; and it exhibits and exposes the relationship between the person being diagnosed and the one doing the diagnosis. Therefore, diagnosis is inherently social in nature, whether it is being done by the psychiatrist, psychologist, sociologist, social worker, or anyone else. Being a social relationship, psychological diagnosis is a political affair! It is a part of the political system!

So, when we see an individual with a disturbed psyche, the individual disturbs our psyche and our mental equilibrium. In the process of diagnosis, it is not only the imbalance of the individual that we are looking at, but at the threat to our own mental balance. The individual then is not only disturbing to his own peace of mind: He is disturbing to our peace, and in more ways than one he is disturbing to our ways of doing things.

Therefore the behavior that we are diagnosing may represent a disturbing questioning of our ways of doing things, our values, and the nature of our social relations. The behavior of the so-called sick individual threatens us, threatens to expose our failures, our hypocrisies, our collusion in bringing about the state of mind of the individual who confronts us. So diagnosis is not a one-way street, where only the patient is looked at. It is a two-way street, where both the patient and the psychiatrist look at each other and work out their problem together, not just the patient's problem.

When we talk about the so-called diagnosing of our people, it involves an analysis not only of the behavior of our people, but of the behavior of the society as a whole; and we must recognize this fact and face up to it as a people. Diagnosis then is not merely procedural or neutral. As we have said, it is political to the core: It is a political act.

Through diagnosis, the ruling society applies its ideological measures to the recalcitrant members of that society. It maintains through diagnosis the status quo, and most of all, through diagnosis, the society — where that society is unjust

— justifies its repressions. Thus, when an individual is labeled in an unjust and unequal society, and is labeled by the very people who maintain its injustice and inequality, then the very diagnostic process itself, and the very labels attached the victims of that society are the very means by which repression is carried out in that system. Consequently, those of us who are in the so-called helping-professions and in the business of diagnosing other people's behavior must recognize the degree to which we are a part of the repressive mechanism of that system.

As the system looks its victims in their faces, as it judges them, it sees its own behavior, its own face in the behavior and face of its victims, and of its patients. The crazy behavior, the face of madness strikes terror in its very soul. That is, the society through its diagnostic procedures looks at the face of its victims, sees the face of its own deviance, the hidden, internal, covert rottenness it represents is externalized and glares back impertinently at it. As D'Amato (N.Y. Senator) said yesterday, he's just intimidated by merely being in the subway in the company of Black people; that merely seeing Black teenagers and people on the street is intimidating. And he is not the only one. Many of us as Black parents and individuals are intimidated as well. We are more frightened by our own children and by our own people than we are by another people — and that is a sad commentary upon our state.

When we see them, they look back at us. But in a sense they show us to ourselves. And we get angry and hostile and we contend, "How dare the victim bleed under the cutting lashes of our social repression? How dare you yell out in pain when we kick your butt? How dare you strike back when we strike you? How dare you protest when we kill your youngsters in the street? How dare you disrupt the court proceedings when we are doing a legal lynching in our courts? How dare you accuse us?" the system asks. And it says, "There is no time to deal with social and political causality. The menace that you people represent must be removed immediately." I find it somewhat amusing that after raping and robbing the world, after killing and destroying, after building weapons that will kill each individual in the world ten times over, after permitting individuals (such as Howard Hughes and others) to be worth billions of dollars while others starve to death, after robbing people day in and day out — *the European thinks he has a right to sleep at night*; that he has the right to walk down the street and feel safe; and has a right to be treated civilly! What kind of fools does he think the people of the world are? What kind of world does he think this is that he can get away with rape and robbery, then expect the victims not to protest in some fashion, form or the other, be that protest self-destructive or otherwise?

But we have a system that asks the so-called helping-professions to "keep *them* away from us; make *them* invisible; convert *their* behavior; make *them* adjust to the system in one way or the other. Use your diagnostic and treatment powers as a means of giving us peace at night!" Thus, "diagnosis" in this context becomes part of the problem. It becomes the means by which the establishment denies its own culpability. It becomes a defense mechanism by which the establishment denies its guilt and defends its self-image and prerogatives. Diagnosis becomes the means by which the establishment projects its criminality and its own insanity onto its victims. Diagnosis is in this instance a mechanism of denial, projection, and repression — both psychical and political.

Through diagnosis the establishment finds what it is looking for. In its criminals it finds evidence of a criminal nature: broken homes; un-caring, rejecting or permissive parents; alcoholic, criminal, or absent fathers; disorganized or ghetto neighborhoods; moral laxities; skewed values. That is to say, in its infinite wisdom and scientific reflection the system finds a criminal type and says: "The criminal-type that we find on the subways generally is one that comes from a broken home, between age thirteen and twenty-five, male, comes from a disorganized community, smokes, and drinks intoxicating liquors. This criminal-type is aggressive, has a weak ego, is hostile, prone to injure his victims for no reason; he is poorly educated, can hardly read, has identity problems; he resists authority, has no respect for the property of others — he is totally hedonistic!" Hence the psychological profile is born. Yes, this may be the kind of criminals that you find in the subways. These may be the kinds of people you find mugging, but does that say that there is a criminal nature existent? Or does it say a criminal nature has been *created* by a system? So then, what the psychologist and the psychiatrist do (ignoring the political social circumstances) is to test the individual, and measure the individual, and find exactly what the society has created...in the name of so-called diagnoses...and the "game" is on.

Diagnosis then becomes individual, just as the ideology which rationalizes the repression of our people is individualistic in nature. Through diagnosis, a preventive program is promulgated. And how do we promulgate the preventive program? We have a program now that says that we want to identify "career-criminals." We are going to arrest the career-criminals, those who have just robbed, and stolen quite often, and when we get them again we are going to lock them up, because, "it's 25 percent of the criminals that produce 75 percent of the crime." Isn't that nice, scientific and neat? Since we are able to diagnose, and looking at our computers determine who is a career-criminal, all we have to do now is go out and arrest them, put them in jails, and then we can sleep at night. Oh, our great criminologists, aren't they wonderful? That may be true. Who's fighting that kind of diagnosis, except that the *root* of the problem is not dealt with. So the system creates the career-criminal, then finds a means of identifying the career-criminal, and then punishes the career-criminal and thereby commits a crime in the name of *law* — and we wonder why the prisons create criminals: Because they are a part of the criminal assault against the people to begin with.

Through diagnosis then, what do we get as a preventive program? More policemen, more retaining of people in the "ghettos", stricter and swifter sentences. We say, "Bring them in today and string them up tomorrow!" "Build more prisons, inject more potent psychotropic drugs, carry weapons to defend yourself, more birth control, more positive images, hold up the Black tokens so that they can learn to mute their behavior while they are striving to make it! More token job training, more government project-housing, more welfare, more summer camps, more fresh-air funds, more P.A.Ls (Police Athletic Leagues)." More of every kind of band-aid solution rather than a fundamental restructuring of the society itself!

So the identity-program, i.e., the program for identifying so-called *career-criminals*, that is supposedly based upon diagnostic technique, is a program that involves everything but a societal self-examination; everything but fundamental social reconstruction; everything but a radical reorganization of social relations. We have more social workers, more psychologists, various and sundry helping-professions. Yet we dare not say the society is sick! How can we say that a society is sick? Only people can be sick. People are society, of course. But I ask you, if the society is not sick — why is it that we have so many psychologists, social workers, and all of the other helping-professions? They must be attending to someone. And we can't get enough of them. We hear again and again — more! more! more! More social workers, more psychologists, psychiatrists, special educators... more! more! This indicates then that society is having some kind of problem. Constantly it demands more people and more professionals who in their very therapeutic relationships with their so-called clients symbolize and maintain the power relations of the society as a whole; who maintain the ethnic relations and the values that are responsible for a good deal of their patients' illnesses in the first place.

Our very so-called therapeutic relationships reflect the class organization of this repressive society — the middle-class interpreting the behavior of the lower-class, the middle-class defining the behavior of the lower-class or those that are "outside" of the society. The administration in this hospital [Harlem Hospital] and all other hospitals of similar nature, reflects the general ethnic structure of our society itself. The administration of rehabilitative centers and other institutions that *supposedly* deal with our children, their very structures themselves represent the structure that drives their clients crazy to begin with — White administrators sitting on top with Black lackeys working on the bottom. So the very essence of their work is undermined by the very structural relationship within the so-called therapeutic environment itself. Hence, the one-on-one, the interpreting, defining, Black counselors using Eurocentric psychodiagnostic ideology see themselves as a part of the society to which they are rendering service.

Therefore, the patient's face is a mirror. And in that face we see our own madness. It mocks us. We feel a compulsion to break it into a thousand pieces. We want to shoot it, and destroy it, because it tells us something we don't want to hear about ourselves. We want to lock them up, and put them away, because they indicate our own failings as a society. We want to chuck it, and make it invisible. The face in the mirror our people reflect, we want to avoid. We diagnose the patient. We see the reflection as a property of the mirror, as a part of its nature. It says nothing about us, we would like to think. In other words then, when we look at the patient we diagnose, we do not wish to admit a reflection of our own responsibility there. We want to say that what is reflected itself represents the nature of the patient.

The Repression of Frankenstein

Diagnosis becomes a prerequisite for the legitimization of repression — psychiatric repression as well as legal and political repression — for the initiation of state-terror. When we talked about *the Eight*, we talked about the other things that are going on in our society, we see diagnosis serving as a means for establishing state-terror; as a means for the transformation of sadistic practices into the practices of rehabilitation, correction, psychiatry and social work. The establishment thus legitimizes its monopoly of the right to incarcerate, torture, harass, maim and kill in order to maintain its order through diagnosis, through the correct and bureaucratic execution of procedure. After careful, thoughtful, precise probing, measuring and testing, *Dr. Frankenstein*, in the name of science and humanity and humanness, labels his own creation a monster, its behavior as monstrous. It possesses no social graces. No, it gets loud on the subway, calls itself by a degrading name for the world to hear, curses, smokes, plays loud music. We see it there. It is brutal, it is dangerous, self-centered, peevish, drinks, smokes a lot, and eats a lot of odd things, just as predicted by the criteria. Its behavior, the conditions of its life correlate highly with our expectations.

And therefore we declare, Dr. Frankenstein declares, if it looks like a monster, if it walks like a monster, if it talks like a monster, then it must be a monster — it fits the monster profile: our tests are valid. And this is ultimately what diagnosis does: *It finds its own creation through the use of Eurocentric diagnostic instruments.* And this not only occurs where there are mental problems, but where there are physical problems. A lot of the physical ills that plague our people are created as a result of dealing with the legal and political repression that is existent in the world order today. Thus we find Dr. Frankenstein creating the monster, diagnosing the monster, then rehabilitating the monster — and ultimately destroying the monster. But who diagnoses Dr. Frankenstein? *Is not the madness of the creature a reflection of the madness of the creator?* Who will rehabilitate Dr. Frankenstein? Who will stop his fiendish experiments?

This is the issue that we have to deal with today as a people.

I would like to say one other thing. There are many of us who say, "those people who mug us, terrorize us on our streets, are Black like us so this is not an ethnic thing. Right? They mug more Black people than they mug White people. And they intimidate Blacks as well as Whites." We cannot deny that as true. It doesn't help for us as a people to deny that as the truth. It doesn't help us as a people to deny the reality of the situation that we are in, and to deny that a sizable percentage of our people are behaving in ways that intimidate not only the so-called White man, but intimidate us as a people. And that reality has to be faced as well, and many of us are reluctant to discuss it.

I don't want to leave you with the impression that we are a passive people who are totally manipulated by a Eurocentric structure, and who are created totally by the White devil. We also as a people must examine ourselves and see to what extent we have participated in the creation of the monster. We must look at the nature and type of leadership we have provided that has helped to maintain this situation, as well. We must look at the responsibility that we have ignored and that we have denied exists as a people. We must look at the opportunities for controlling ourselves and for developing a different kind of people. Therefore, it is not only the White man who cannot sleep at night; we also are not able to sleep at night either, because a part of the situation that we face is also our responsibility as well.

We must look at the assimilationist leadership that we have permitted to represent us in this world today. We must look at the kind of leadership that always has had its face turned outward, towards the White man, and neglected the education of the re-socialization of our own people; a leadership who has spent its energies trying to convert the White man, instead of, in part, using that energy for converting ourselves as a people. For we are not only the creation of an evil European — we, in part, have helped to create the European.

The Power of Self-Transformation

As noted by Chancellor Williams (*The Destruction of Black Civilization*), the way we think, the way we behave, helps to create the kinds of victimization from which we suffer. The oppressive configuration the White man has assumed in relationship to the Black man is in good part the result of the fact that we have permitted ourselves to remain in a complementary subordinate configuration conducive to his oppressive designs. *The White man cannot be what he is unless we are what we are as a people.* And one way of transforming the White man is through *self-transformation*. He cannot be what he is if we are not what we are. Therefore, we must take responsibility for that part of our personality, that part of our community, and that part of ourselves over which we have control, and change that part. And if we change those parts of ourselves and our community we shall change this man. Who gives a damn about changing him anyway? It does not matter!

One of our major problems is that Black leadership has been involved in converting Whites. That misleads us time and time again. Give it up! One of the major steps in the rehabilitation of the Black man is to give up the White man and forget about him!

I see children, and I see people who are crazy, blaming their mothers: "She didn't love me; she rejected me; she never hugged me; she never kissed me. I was the darker one, and she liked the lighter one." And we get story after story, and justification after justification, and the person remains in his/her craziness waiting for the other person, *mama*, to change. And the surprising thing about it is that — if mama changed you'd still be crazy as you were before — because the energy dissipated waiting and trying to change mama has been diverted, and the energy needed for self-change has atrophied, and therefore, even when the opportunity presents itself the personality is unable to take advantage of it. The Black community must examine itself and see to what degree it has contributed to its own madness, demise, oppression and powerlessness.

A part of the problem of mental illness is not what people do to each other, and not what mama, or daddy, or somebody else does to a child. A part of it is also how what mama does is reacted to on the part of the child. It is not so much that the European says we are inferior, and that we are this and that, and that the European maligns our character, et cetera: *It is the belief on our part that what he says is true that drives us crazy.* It is a crazy reaction to what he says, an insane and unthinking kind of approach to dealing with what he says about us, that maintains the craziness. It is the reaction of anger, as Cobbs and Price points out, "the reaction of rage." Yes, we are going to find rage in teenagers, and rage in people that destroy and prey on the community: and it is this reaction that distorts reality, distorts the individual's creativity, distorts the necessary unity and distorts the very mechanism that can get the individual out of his/her behavior.

I was talking to one drug addict who was outlining the regular thing about mama; mama not loving her and mama mistreating her. And so she saw herself as having *only* two choices: either she would become what mama said she would become, or she would become better than what mama said she would become — both being reactions to mama, both still tied her to mama, both making her a creation of mama. The Black bourgeoisie is as much a creation as is the Black criminal; they are both reactionary styles, and both a means by which a people try to deal with the dilemma of White oppression. And quite often people think, (and she thought) that there are only two choices: Either I react to it that way or I react to it the other way; I react to it in terms of rage or I overachieve. But if reactions of rage, and hatred, and vengeance are not permitted to capture the personality, to consume and concentrate consciousness and attention, perhaps then, another alternative, another approach will be discovered. This is the thing that we must recognize in ourselves as a people. Reactions in terms of depression, rage and anger, reactions in terms of compensatory mechanisms, are reactions that help to deny the criminality on a certain segment of our people, and that obscures the behavior of many of our teenagers in our current situation — which help to maintain the situation in and of itself.

The problems confronting Black people did not just occur under Ronald Reagan. The dis-employment of Black people is not something that just occurred under Ronald Reagan. They have been there all along — since we touched foot in the New World and the European set foot on the lands of Afrikan peoples.

Why can't leadership deal with that issue? Why is it we say that Black people are losing out in the so-called "alms" race, as they call it? ALMS race! Why aren't we questioning our leadership when, since the 1950s — after our "great victory" in the Supreme Court — the situation of our people is worsening? We have a leadership that refuses to confront forthrightly the issues and the circumstances in which we find ourselves. For that we must hold ourselves responsible. For the madness and disorganization that flows from that, we must hold ourselves responsible. For not capturing economic and social control of our communities, and for not building up Pan-Afrikanism, and for not building up our brains, and studying, and reading, and writing, and organizing, and developing, we must hold ourselves responsible, in part, for the madness. I therefore suggest that the issue then is not so much one of diagnosis of the patient, but a diagnosis of ourselves, a diagnosis of the system, and more so than that — getting on with the work of revolution.

Endnotes

a. The case of the *New York Eight* involves a group of Afrikan Americans of the Black liberation movement arrested in "preemptive" raids across Brooklyn, Queens and Manhattan on October 19, 1984, by the NYPLD/FBI Joint Terrorist Task Force.

After 22 months of physical and electronic surveillance, the *Eight* were arrested just 5 days after the Preventive Detention Act (no bail law) was instituted. When a judge ruled this law did not apply to the *Eight*, subpoenas for voice and writing exemplars were issued — despite 700 hours of taped conversation and several handwriting samples seized in the October arrests. Though as of Feb 2, 1985, they were yet to be charged with a crime, they had been in and out of prison.

"Preventive Detention," part of a Comprehensive Crime Control Act 1984, provides for detention without bail — prior to being adjudged guilty in a federal court — on the premise that the defendant is a substantial risk to flee subsequent to making bail or is a threat to the public if released.

See also *Big Red* newspaper of Feb 2, 1985. pg. 3.
See also *Amsterdam News* of December 1, 1984. pg. 1.

Part Three

THE
POLITICAL
PSYCHOLOGY
OF
BLACK
CONSCIOUSNESS

III

Sociopathology precedes psychopathology. Collective pathology precedes individual pathology. That is, *dis*eased social interactions *between* groups generate *dis*eased social interactions *within* groups, and furthermore, *dis*eased social interactions within groups generate *dis*eased psychological interactions *within* individuals who are their constituents. The discontents of individuals reflect the discontents of groups; and these, the discontents of the societies and cultures they constitute. The Great Chain of Discontents inextricably binds together individual, group, society, and culture.

The character and conduct of groups and individuals however labeled and categorized, whether judged to be good or evil, superior or inferior, are the products of historic intergroup, intragroup, and interpersonal relations, and can only be meaningfully understood in terms of these relations. The character and behavior of Afrikan American individuals, whether labeled "normal" or "abnormal," can only be fully and accurately comprehended, along with the process and purpose of labeling itself, in terms of the historic power relations between dominant European-American and subordinate Afrikan-American groups.

White domination and Black subordination involve special types of social power relations constructed predominantly by Whites in order that they might receive certain material and non-material benefits thereby. These social power relations involve social practices and processes which mediate the White American socioeconomic, sociopolitical, sociopsychological manipulation and construction of Black consciousness and behavior. Under White supremacy Black consciousness and behavior are socially manufactured, labeled, and judged by

Whites in ways consonant with their social control and expropriation of Black natural and acquired human resources. The *"normality"* or *"abnormality"* of Black consciousness and behavior are so classified with reference to the degree to which they support or oppose to the continuity of White supremacy. "Normal" Black consciousness and behavior under the various regimes of White domination are characterized by habitual thought patterns and behavioral tendencies which render them pliable to White authoritarian/authoritative social control with minimal resistance; which induce Blacks to accept their subordinate status as natural, perhaps actually to misperceive their oppression as freedom. "Abnormal" Black consciousness and behavior under White supremacy involve habitual thought patterns and behavioral tendencies in Blacks which make their social control by Whites intolerably difficult or ineffective; which induces them to protest, resist and reject their subordinate status as destined or natural, to perceive their oppression as unfreedom.

From the vantage point of the continuity of White supremacy, the basis for the labeling of Black consciousness and behavior by Whites as normal or abnormal depends not on the discovery by Whites of discrete states of consciousness and their correlated behavioral tendencies in Blacks, but on the discovery of the degree to which Black consciousness/behavioral tendencies are perceived as serving or dis-serving their hegemonic interests.

Disturbances of thought, emotions, motivational and values priorities, and psychological processes in Blacks are the unavoidable outcomes of their oppression by Whites. To be oppressed is by definition to have one's thought processes disturbed; emotions impaired; motives and values inverted; and one's body functions imbalanced. There can be no "normality" of consciousness and conduct for Blacks as long as they remain dominated by Whites — merely socially acceptable or unacceptable adjustments to the ever-changing demand characteristics of White supremacy. The normality of Blacks under White domination is by that circumstance, above all, a "pathological normalcy" — disturbances in Black consciousness and behavior which are deemed serviceable and beneficial to the needs of their White oppressors.

The alleged normality or abnormality of Black consciousness under White supremacy requires that Blacks involuntarily and obsessively deceive themselves. This collective self-deception, which is the benchmark of oppressed Black consciousness, is the main product of White-Black social power relations, motivated by anxiety and ignorance, founded on the denial and distortion of reality. Both the normality and abnormality of Black consciousness and behavior as reproduced by the power relations of White supremacy, also require that they operate against their own best interests in the interests of their White oppressors; that they be self-denying, self-defeating, and oft-times self-destructing, while convincing themselves that the opposite is true.

Normality is as much a political-economic concept as a psychological-social concept. As a political/economic construct it is the result, in large part, of the interplay of intergroup, intragroup and primary group social-economic power relations and practices which have been exercised on the bodies of persons. Normality is born of fairly systemic methods of rewarding and punishing behavior, ritual practices and indoctrination, training, correction, supervision, and constraint. As societies change so do their fields of power relations, methods of socialization, and concepts of normalcy. To paraphrase Foucault,[5] the "normality" which inhabits a person and brings him into existence is itself a factor in the mastery that those in power exercise over that person's consciousness and behavior. Normality as a functional state of being, as a circumscribed set of states of consciousness and their correlated behavioral tendencies, is the effect and instrument of dynamic political-economic relations. The "norm" is in essence a principle of coercion; a constraint on behavior; a rule to be followed. It involves the establishment of a set of values or standards, a

---

[5] Foucault, M. 1979. *Discipline and Punishment: The Birth of the Prison.* New York: Vintage Books.

range of behaviors to be respected which must be achieved through conformity, reinforced by social sanctions, rewards, and punishments. *Normalization*, the process of using the values of the norm to compare, differentiate, hierarchize, homogenize; to determine the level and value of abilities and the "nature" of persons and groups; to exclude; to mark the frontier of the abnormal — and thereby ration power, privilege and favor — is one of the great instruments of power wielded by those who rule and dominate others. Hence, under White supremacy the "normality" of Blacks is to a significant extent both the effect and the instrument of White power. For the subordinated Afrikan, "normality" is the prison of his mind and body.

Labeling As Social Control

As noted earlier, both "normal" and "abnormal" states of consciousness and their correlated behavioral tendencies in oppressed Afrikans provide the means and justification for their social control by dominant Europeans, who claim an exclusive license for defining and labeling such states. These consciousness/behavioral states once ordered and reordered by oppression, are rationalized and reversed by the mental health establishment in ways that their effects are made to appear to be causes. Under oppression the process of labeling behavior is as much a part of the problem as it claims to be a part of the solution. For the labeling process obscures the purposes for and means by which those states labeled are generated, maintained, and changed to fit the needs of those in power. The labeling process is then no longer only demarcative but is also generative, i.e., the process itself helps to generate states of consciousness as well as denote them.

The authority to label consciousness and behavior reflects social power inequalities between the labelers and the labeled. Therefore, the authority to label is a central factor in the processes of social power and often functions to maintain or increase power inequalities. Labeling behavior as normal or abnormal may contribute to maintaining or enhancing prevailing power inequalities in that by directing attention to their purported intrapsychic, subcultural or genetic sources, the causal relevance of other social, political, economical phenomena in generating and maintaining such behavior are down-played, dismissed or obscured.

Labeling and defining behavior is a part of a power-rationing process in which certain segments of a society are granted exclusive legitimacy and power to explain, diagnose and treat certain states of consciousness and forms of behavior not granted to others. The process of granting such exclusive rights may be referred to as the granting of authority to the recipient person or group. Based on custom, competence, other legal precedence, or codes, the authority is granted a socially acknowledged right to command the compliance of others under specified circumstances.

Authority is not merely ascribed or granted to a particular person or social group in a society for pragmatic reasons alone. The social and political ascription or granting of authority is usually rationalized or legitimated in terms of an underlying ideology. Once the ideology which rationalizes and legitimates a particular authority structure gains general social acceptance and the political approbation of the ruling regime, it not only tends to delegitimize alternative or opposing ideologies but also tends to empower and legitimate the ruling regime along with those who control its operational apparatus. This may occur in spite of the rather obvious failure of the ideology and the authority structure it legitimates to adequately explain, resolve or significantly ameliorate, the problems they were ostensibly established to explain or resolve (e.g., the criminal justice or mental health establishment along with their legitimating ideologies).

When a ruling regime, e.g., the White supremacist establishment, persists in maintaining an ideological-authority structure in power in spite of its apparent dysfunctionality (i.e., as measured by its inability to resolve its assigned problems) one may infer from this the possibility that that ideological-authority structure's real, but obscured, function may be primarily to help to rationalize, legitimate, and maintain the ruling regime's social order and power relations. It achieves these ends by attempting to define and resolve its assigned problems in ways which do not indict the regime and its operational structure as the probable causes of the problems to begin with (because the presence of such problems may be utilized to actually help to justify, preserve, and empower the ruling regime).

Domination and the Mislabeling of Behavior

Domination as a social fact and situation necessarily disorders and reorders the thoughts, feelings, emotions, motivations, values, psychological states, and consequently, the consciousness and behavior of the dominated. This disordering and reordering of consciousness and behavior necessarily involve their politically functional labeling and classification by their instigators. Classifying and labeling the consciousness and behavior of the oppressed by their oppressors provide the means by which the abnormality and pathology generated by oppression are "normalized" in the oppressed, i.e., made to appear to follow the natural order of the universe. The normalization of pathology is exquisitely functional for oppressive regimes. It is for this productive reason that oppressive White supremacy always attempts to rationalize its oppression of Blacks by normalizing their reactionary, pathological, Eurocentric consciousness and behavior and simultaneously abnormalizing both the reactionary and proactionary, non-pathological and pathological Afrocentric consciousness and behavior with regard to their political-economic functionality for maintaining White dominance. In its attempts to normalize oppression the oppressive White supremacist regime seeks to deceptively, yet convincingly, demonstrate that the modal consciousness and behavior of subordinated Afrikans represent the spontaneous, natural, and normal products of original Afrikan character and culture. Thus under White supremacy the concept of the normal, abnormal and the pathological in human consciousness and behavior is relativized — i.e., defined in terms of the degree to which they are or are not supportive of White domination.

The Medicalization of Afrikan Social Problems

A prime and relevant example of the construction of an ideological-authority structure by a ruling regime (White supremacy) in order to maintain its social status quo is the rapidly expanding medicalization of the "deviant behavior," e.g., criminality, academic problems, of Afrikan Americans. That is, problems which may be accurately defined as derivative of ethnic, social, political, economic, personal conflicts and dislocations are defined as derivative of biological malformations and imbalances. As comprehensively defined by Conrad (1980), the medicalization of deviant or anti-social behavior refers to:

> ...the defining and labeling of deviant behavior as a medical problem, an illness, and mandating the medical profession to provide some type of treatment for it. Concomitant with this is the growing utilization of medicine as an agent of social control, typically as medical intervention. Medical intervention as social control seeks to limit, modify, regulate, isolate or eliminate socially defined deviant behavior, *with medical means and in the name of health.*[6]

The medicalization of socially and politically deviant behavior as ideology depoliticizes such behavior by denying its political origins and causality and by refusing to consider its remediation and prevention through the implementation of appropriate political, economic and social reconstructions. Through medicalization deviant behavior is "biologized," "ethnicized" and "geneticized," that is, viewed as indicative of isolated, individual aberrations of body and brain balances, or of inherited racial proclivities, genetic shortcomings or deficiencies. The medicalization of many types of criminal, anti-social, deficient, and maladaptive behavior by Afrikans in America permits the ruling White supremacist regime to deny that its

---

[6] Conrad, Peter. "Medicalization of deviants and social control" in David Ingleby (ed.) *Critical Psychiatry: The Politics of Mental Health* N.Y.: Pantheon Books, 1980.

social, political, racist and economic policies and practices are very significantly responsible for much of the occurrence of such behavior. Instead, the blame is passed on to the victims themselves by labeling them "mentally ill," "organically deficient," and in need of surveillance, detention, isolation, rehabilitation, behavior modification, and/or medication — not of political-economic redress.

Even when social causation is allowed by the medical ideological-authority structure, the causal chain usually begins and ends by blaming the patient's, client's or deviant's family, primary and peer group relations and subcultural particularities as the primary sources of his problems. Rarely is the over-arching political-economic-cultural regime which significantly helps to determine the expressive character of those relations and particularities considered or critically analyzed. Moreover, the reigning therapeutic "treatment" approach may still be couched in medical terminology, executed in clinical-institutional settings, and the patient's maladjustment alleviated by medicinal or "ethnicized psychotherapy."

Ethnicized Psychotherapy

Ethnicized psychotherapy may include non-medicalized or non-psychiatric approaches to the "correction" of behavioral misconduct by using various therapeutic labeling, treatment, or behavior modification procedures to return the deviant to normalcy," i.e., to ..."the norms of one group — those with established power and a vested interest in resisting social change — [norms] declared to be the norms of society as a whole."[7] In this instance what is considered normal is also considered necessarily good and moral. In contrast the abnormal or deviant is considered bad and immoral. In this guise ethnicized psychotherapy may be rightly perceived as an ally of medicalized psychotherapy in that they both provide practical benefits to the ruling establishment by advancing its estab-

---

[7] Heather, N. 1976. *Radical Perspectives in Psychology*. London: Methuen.

lished moral and political positions against those of the oppressed disguised as humane, enlightened, disinterested and apolitical therapeutics. Thus, what at first sight may appear to be the utilization of an objective, scientific approach in dealing with deviancy in reality involves the stigmatization, moral condemnation and politicization of the behavior and consciousness of people or persons struggling against social injustice and inequality.

Ronald Leifer (1969) defined the ethnicization of psycho-therapy "as the molding and the polarization of behavior so that it conforms to prevailing cultural patterns. It is indoctrination or training for culturally specific traits, attitudes, and actions."[8] The aim of ethnicized psychotherapy is to return the deviant to "normal," i.e., to instill in the deviant a set of particular traits, attitudes, values, behavioral orientations, and goals which when pursued or realized, support and maintain the political-economic social status quo along with its ruling elite.

Ethnicized psychotherapy, like its medicalized counterpart, also strips "...the deviant act of its social [and political] meaning by presenting it as mechanistically or in some other way determined, [thereby denying] ...that the act could possibly be justified from the standpoint of an alternative view of social morality" (Heather, 1976). Ethnicized psychotherapy, too, views any form of behavior and state of consciousness which do not conform to the norms or political-economic interests of the ruling establishment or group as, "by definition, a reflection of individual maladjustment, emotional immaturity, mental pathology, or some other negatively valued concept" (Heather, 1976). Thus, problems which may be reflective of social and political problems are dismissed as the ailments of isolated individuals, as evidence of individual maladjustment, the epiphenomena of a distorted personality — all abstracted from the field of social and economic forces which generate their existence and form.

---

[8] Leifer, R. 1969. *In the Name of Mental Health: The Social Functions of Psychiatry.* New York: Science House.

Ethnicized psychotherapy, like medicalized psychotherapy, either exhibits a lack of interest in comprehending the behavior and consciousness of persons and groups from the point of view of their real political, social, and cultural history; or exhibits an exclusive, narrow interest in comprehending their behavior and consciousness in terms of something *inside* them — some inner dynamic formed in early childhood; in terms of purported family or subcultural dynamics; inherited "traits," or "conditioned responses" — all originating in some purely personalized or isolated group history. Consequently, the complex system of social and economic forces constructed and manipulated by the ruling group which constrains and restricts the consciousness of subordinate groups by setting limits in the form of laws, biased discriminations, degrading expectations, sheer economic and political repressions — is ignored and the pathogenic social order it regulates is thereby *maintained.*

The "ethnicized" therapist is empowered and employed by the ruling group to create or modify various mental-behavioral orientations into his or her client which are compatible with its power needs and political-economic culture. Through the therapeutic encounter the client is conditioned to politically respond to prefabricated social directives and sign-stimuli which organize and direct his or her perceptions, feelings, thoughts and actions along certain political lines and to accord with certain political-economic ends. Often the therapeutic, rehabilitative, or in a broader sense, educative encounter attempts to induce in the client the belief that it is in his or her best interest to think and behave in ways compatible with the needs of the dominant group which the therapeutic or educative therapist represents. This aim is achieved through the therapist's formulation of the goals of therapy, education, or rehabilitation for the client and the setting of conditions for the client's social conduct in general.

Educative Psychotherapy

Leifer (1969) makes an important distinction between ethnicized psychotherapy and educative psychotherapy. He points out that both therapeutic approaches turn on the fulcrum of social power. He contends that, "Ethnicization involves the *use* of social power to influence thought and conduct in socially approved directions. Education involves the *analysis* of social power, among other subjects, to understand its influence on the lives of individuals and social groups."

Given the political-economic position of Afrikans in the world today and the negative social and mental health outcomes devolving therefrom, an Afrikan-centered educational and therapeutic psychology emphasizes critical analysis and understanding of how the ethnicizing Eurocentric social agent, whether therapist, educator, etc., attempts to mold Afrikan behavior to fit specific eurocentrically self-serving legal, moral, political, and ethnic standards. An Afrikan-centered educative approach in addition to defining and designating certain states of consciousness and forms of behavior relative to the needs of Afrikan peoples, must engage the client in a full analysis of his life goals and methods for achieving them while helping to imbue his efforts with social meaning, purpose, and creative power. It seeks to imbue in its participants an Afrikan-centered consciousness and behavioral orientation which will maximize the positive expression of his fundamental humanity and his ability to maximally contribute to the growth and development of the Afrikan community of which he is a member.

The participant in Afrikan-centered therapeutic and educational encounters discovers how he has been unconsciously conditioned by a Eurocentric system to respond habitually and unthinkingly to its social cues to Eurocentric authorities and social contexts which induce him "to perceive, think, feel, and behave in certain ways, ...how he has been cued *to avoid* perceiving, thinking, feeling, and behaving in certain ways" (Leifer, 1969); how his Eurocentric consciousness, the source of his domination, is but a state of unconsciousness representing itself as consciousness. Eurocentric consciousness, the mortal enemy of Afrikan-centered consciousness which it displaces and represses, imposes on its Afrikan hosts the dream states of sleepwalkers and somnambulistic wanderers in the dark of night.

A major educative, therapeutic and politically liberating milestone is reached in Afrikan-centered therapy and education when the participants, be they labeled normal or abnormal, conformists or deviants, become poignantly aware of how the various institutions and practices which define Eurocentric culture are utilized to control Afrikan people's minds and behavior; prevent Afrikans from developing the social skills and knowledge necessary for them to be masters of their own destiny; foster the kinds of behavioral ineptitudes and deviations often labeled as "deficient," "anti-social" or "mental illness"; maintain Afrikan unawareness of the social games and rules by which that culture transforms and dominates Afrikan consciousness and behavior; condition Afrikans to avoid thinking and behaving in ways which expand their self-consciousness and behavioral repertoire; impair Afrikans' ability to master their own conduct, increase their self-reliance and self-sufficiency; impair their ability to acquire the intellectual and social skills, the critical intelligence to solve the problems of their lives, the material and capacities to determine their own future intelligently.

Afrikan peoples can best successfully counter the hegemonic interests of Eurocentric society by reclaiming their Afrikan-centered consciousness, identity and social interest; by founding their consciousness and behavior on an accurate perception of, and respect for, reality and a passionate love of truth; on a knowledge and acceptance of their Afrikan heritage; a dedicated passion to achieve and maintain conscious, thoughtful, voluntary self-control; their ability to first love themselves; to maintain affectionate relations and positive regard among themselves; the achievement of a collective, cooperative, unifying consciousness and behavioral orientation and; on the ability to engage in productive prosocial, proactive, rather than counterproductive, self-defeating, reactionary, activities. However, these objectives will not be attained until Afrikan empowerment neutralizes or reverses the power relations and differentials which are the social foundations of White supremacy.

Fighting the Power

The ability of dominant Whites to socially manufacture or markedly influence Afrikan states of consciousness and conduct in the interest of perpetuating White supremacy, is both the source and product of the power relations and inequalities which inhere between these races. The White social manufacture of Black consciousness and behavior will end when the power differentials which make this process possible are equalized or reversed by the increased Black empowerment. This necessary equation or reversal of power relations begins when Afrikans come to understand the nature of power, its social origins and applications; when they recognize that they are as capable of its acquisition and disposition as are their European (and other ethnic group) counterparts; and when they consciously and deliberately choose to acquire and dispose of it in their own interests and in the defense of their own liberty. The Afrikan understanding and application of power must begin with a pragmatic concept of power such as outlined by Foucault:

> [P]ower...is conceived not as a property, but as a strategy, that its effects of domination are attributed not to 'appropriation', but to dispositions, maneuvers, tactics, techniques, functionings; that one should decipher in it a network of relations, constantly in tension, in activity, rather than a privilege that one might possess; that one should take as its model a perpetual battle rather than a contract regulating a transaction or the conquest of a territory. In short, this *power is exercised rather than possessed; it is not the 'privilege', acquired or preserved, of the dominant class, but the overall effect of its strategic positions* — an effect that is manifested and sometimes extended by the position of those who are dominated.[9] (Emphasis added).

The strategies and tactics by which dominant Whites attempt to order, re-order and disorder Afrikan consciousness and behavior must be neutralized by Afrikan-centered strategic and

---

[9] Ibid.

tactical counterattacks. The metaphysical preparation to undertake such countermoves first must include the thorough decolonizing of Afrikan consciousness and the strategic organization of the Afrikan community, making it capable of creating a collective intelligence and adaptational talent which in turn will enable it to overthrow White supremacy and achieve its liberation from oppression. The very brief outline which follows suggests some broad means by which these goals can be reached.

Reintegration of Afrikan history. The true history and culture of Afrikan peoples must be *re*discovered, *re*examined, and *re*integrated by Afrikan peoples. These approaches to Afrikan history and culture must conjointly become the vehicles which facilitate the collective and cooperative action of Afrikan peoples in the pursuit of their liberation. The appropriate reclamation of Afrikan history and culture will provide Afrikans with a realistic and supportive vision of reality; with self-knowledge, self-esteem, self-confidence, self-acceptance and self-control; with the ability to form empowering affectionate relationships and the ability to engage in proactive, self-interested productive activity; and with a self-enhancing sense of purpose and existential meaningfulness.

An appropriate understanding of Afrikan history and culture will provide Afrikans with an honest, accurate appraisal of their strengths and needs as well as those of their European counterparts. Such an understanding will allow them to discover the strategic and tactical means of liberating themselves from White supremacy.

Upgrading of Coping Resources. The economic organization of the Afrikan community much more so than its alleged economic impoverishment and dependency, in tandem with the repression of its Afrikan-centered consciousness and identity, are principally responsible for its vulnerability to the stresses placed on it by the dominant White supremacist establishment. Because its economic institutions and resources are primarily owned, controlled, and exploited by aliens the Afrikan American community has not been able to finance and construct the necessary social institutions to educate, train and generally socialize its constituents and provide them with the personal and social competencies which together could successfully mediate, resist, and finally overcome the hegemonic intentions of White supremacy. In the spirit of Black nationalism the Afrikan community must occupy and control its internal markets and resources and utilize the resulting proceeds to remediate and finance its entry into national and international markets. This must be accomplished simultaneously with the rapid and effective Afrikan-centered education and socialization of all of its constituents, young and old. The combination of relative economic independence, power and prestige, Afrikan-centered cultural organization and identity, high levels of personal and social competence, will provide quality coping resources which will not only optimize Afrikan mental and social health but will also facilitate Afrikan liberation.

Neutralizing of Social Stressors. Institutional racism generates stressors — such as inadequate family incomes, health care, education, job training, housing, employment, economic development, and restricted, stereotypically-biased information and entertainment services — which strain the Black community's coping mechanisms. The effects of these stressors are amplified by the relatively dependent and reactive orientation of the Afrikan community. The virtual absence of a robust, independent movement in the community leaves it vulnerable to being exploited and victimized by predatory aliens, further increasing its vulnerability to stresses of all types.

The injurious effects of oppression-related stressors on the Afrikan American community would be markedly attenuated if it joins and leads the worldwide Afrikan community in creating an effective economic-cultural bloc so as to advance the interests of Afrikan peoples as equals with other great peoples in the world. The Afrikan community must perceive oppression-related stress as a problem to be solved, as a manageable challenge and a heroic opportunity rather than an overpowering, onerous burden. It can overthrow the weight of White supremacy by engaging in a thorough, painstakingly honest and revolutionary self-critical analysis of the cognitive, emotional, social, informational, linguistic-communicational, economical, physical, and environmental barriers which help to maintain its political-economic subordination. It is well within the power of the Black community to achieve these ends. It needs only to discover and assert its will to power.

Reversing Reactionary States of the Afrikan "Body Politic." The Afrikan body politic must immerse itself in the center of an Afrikan-centered political-economic-historico-cultural force field if it is to repel the sustained hold on it by White supremacy. This can be accomplished by investing the Afrikan body politic with its natural Afrikan-centered knowledge, consciousness and identity. The Afrikan body politic must be rescued from its Eurocentric prisons, denuded of its Eurocentric markings, sensibilities, tastes and appetites, restored to mental and physical health, and trained to do and produce for self.

The energy of the Afrikan body politic must be redirected from its exhaustive expenditure in the construction and maintenance of reactionary psychosocial defenses and damage-control devices to the construction and maintenance of an Afrikan-centered problem-solving consciousness and identity and an indomitable sense of mission. The enormous energy to which the Afrikan body politic is host must be directed toward growth and the creation of opportunities for its positive expression; toward the development of problem-solving and self-actualizing mental-behavioral competencies for successfully mediating and overcoming the stresses of White supremacy.

Controlling of Effective Coping Strategies and Tactics. Afrikans must choose coping strategies and tactics which reverse tendencies to be motivated by eurocentrically induced lacks, deprivations, needs, anxieties, and appetites. The obsessive pursuit and compulsive consumption of psychological, social and physical analgesics, anesthetics, pain relievers, stimulants and euphoriants, as well as the use of addictive social practices as coping strategies against oppression-related stress, must be rejected and replaced by positive, Afrikan-centered practices, pursuits and pleasures. This can be best achieved by the development of community power which produces knowledge and fields of knowledge which simultaneously constitute fields of power relations — power-knowledge relations which will enable the Afrikan community to empower and liberate itself. It must become a community which deeply studies and teaches to its young power-knowledge relations, imaginative, creative, strategic and tactical organization as the keys to power and self-defense.

To be free the Afrikan community must continue and strengthen its tradition of truth-seeking. For the liberation of the community depends on its ability to discern the real sources and causes of its trials and tribulations from both within and outside itself; its ability to solve its problems based on sound knowledge; on objective appraisals of its situation, and on its intuitive and well-developed ability to undertake conscious, rational, and constructive courses of action.

The Afrikan Control of Labeling and Treatment Processes. Paulo Freire[10] has noted that, "Indeed, the interests of the oppressors lie in changing the consciousness of the oppressed, not the situation which oppresses them"; "for the more the oppressed can be led to adapt to that situation, the more easily they can be dominated". Oppressors produce a consciousness in the oppressed not only by manipulating their ecological and sociological lifestyles and possibilities but also by naming the world in which both they and the oppressed exist. To name, to label, is to bring into consciousness and therefore to transform consciousness. In empowering themselves to name the world and to reinforce their naming of it, oppressors empower themselves to construct the social reality and the consciousness of the oppressed in ways compatible with their interests. The social reality and consciousness of the oppressed as forged by their oppressors, motivate them to functionally

---

[10] Freire, P. 1983. *Pedagogy of the Oppressed.* New York: Continuum.

perpetuate their own oppression. The labeling of certain aspects of reality by oppressors represents the imposition of the oppressors' choice and worldview upon the oppressed. If this choice and worldview are internalized by the oppressed, then their consciousness may be transformed into one that confirms their oppressors' consciousness. Through its demarcation of reality the White supremacist regime seeks to transform Afrikan people's consciousness and behavior, as well as their self-perception of their own behavior in ways compatible with Eurocentric interests. The Eurocentric demarcation of reality is not only designed to transform Afrikan behavior and self-perception but to manage the perception that others have of Afrikans as well.

We have intimated that under the aegis of White supremacy the categorizing of behaviors exhibited by Blacks is an especially subtle and effective form of social control. To invest these behaviors with categorical names indicative of mental "illness" allows the White supremacist establishment to divest such categories of behavior of any political significance. The alleged psychopathological symptoms exhibited by Blacks under the alienating processes of White domination are thereby construed as resulting from an intrapsychic or a biogenetic disease process rather than as resulting from their attempts to cope with the alienating effects of White supremacy. Consequently, the "correction" or remediation of deviancy in Blacks centers around the perfection of diagnostic techniques and innovations in therapeutic treatment rather than around making the necessary more effective, innovative changes in cultural lifestyles which will expand the political-economic power and independence of Afrikan peoples. We know that current Eurocentric diagnostic, labeling and treatment processes together provide a thinly-veiled ideological smoke screen for rationalizing and obscuring the processes of domination; provide in the name of health, psychological, social and medical interventions as social control mechanisms for maintaining White-defined Black behavioral conventionality and; provide rationales for the restriction, regulation, isolation, elimination, or modification of Black deviant behavior in terms of its effects on the efficiency of the White-dominated national and global economy.

If this situation is to be transformed to enable subordinate Afrikans to achieve liberation from White domination, then the license to name the world, to categorize, classify, or otherwise demarcate the world and behavior on the part of Whites, must by revoked. Afrikans *must* assert their right and power of self-definition — of categorizing and classifying the world and the nature of their being in it; of prescribing treatments for their behavior and establishing the conditions of their lives — in ways which make their minds and bodies humanitarian instruments of Afrikan power and liberation as well as instruments for the empowerment and liberation from oppression of all humankind.

Appendix

THE NORMALITY AND ABNORMALITY of Black consciousness and behavior as politically mandated and socially manufactured by the power relations of White supremacy, are denoted by the relative prominence of certain disturbances of thought, emotions, motivations and values. These disturbances of consciousness serve the interests of White hegemony by making Blacks highly responsive, for better or worse, to White-instigated social controls. A few examples will suffice to illustrate the point.

The following figure provides some of the common symptoms of *"pathological normalcy"* in Blacks, i.e., those disturbances of thought, emotions, motivations and values which in Blacks are instigated and maintained by the White supremacist establishment in order to sustain its "normal" social order and relations. If exhibited by Whites themselves these symptoms would be immediately adjudged "mental disorders" by the White mental health establishment. Recall that "pathological normalcy" in Blacks refers to those disturbances in Black consciousness and behavior which are beneficial to the needs of Whites and to the perpetuation of White supremacy while being ultimately inimical to their own needs and liberation. These disturbances within the context of White supremacy are either unobserved or adjudged by the White mental health establishment as "normal" or at least, "non-pathological" (because they are compatible with the interests of White supremacy). It is only when the disturbances are of such character, intensity or pervasiveness that they negate the usual or customary social controls and threaten the established social order are they deemed by the White mental health establishment as "abnormal," maladaptive, or "pathological."

COMMON SYMPTOMS OF "PATHOLOGICAL NORMALCY" IN OPPRESSED AFRIKANS

Symptoms Reflecting Thought Disturbances

Amnesia   total or partial loss of memory. A dissociative reaction, occurs when an individual represses from consciousness the recall or remembrance of entire periods or episodes in his life in order to deny, escape, avoid the re-experiencing of certain painful feelings associated with those periods or episodes. Amnesia therefore results in the loss of pre-trauma identity, the motives and values related to that identity due to the repression of its relevant, crucially defining memories.

White supremacy is to a large extent founded on the social amnesia of subordinate Blacks. The ruling White supremacist regime's strategic need to deprive a massive Afrikan population of a common cultural platform from whence to mount a collective counterattack against its domination requires that it negates their common Afrikan identity, cultural, historical memories and related practices. This eradication of Afrikan cultural/ historical memories was (is) undertaken so as to make possible the social manufacture or fashioning of an erstwhile Afrikan identity which can be reactively shaped and molded to fit the ongoing needs and interests of White supremacy. The subordinate Afrikan can only be what he needs to be for dominant Whites if he has no true knowledge of who he is and how he came to be who he is. This requires that he not remember who he truly was. The operative oppression of Blacks by Whites depends on the ability of Whites to create and maintain a discrepancy between what subordinate Afrikans *think* they were and what they truly were; what they perceive themselves to be and what they truly are; what they think they should be and what they must be. These discrepancies are the foundation stones upon which the superstructure of White supremacy is constructed. The reclamation of their true history, cultural continuity and unalloyed identity by Afrikans would

121

precipitate the ruinous collapse of White hegemony. Thus, in self-defense and in the interest of self-perpetuation the White supremacist establishment is compelled to induce and maintain in Black consciousness a pervasive social amnesia regarding things positively Afrikan — an amnesia which is ostensibly "normal."

Social amnesia in subordinate Afrikans was (is) socially manufactured by dominant Whites through the propagandistic slander and falsification of Afrikan history and culture by constricting the continuing discovery, effective exposition, and self-actualizing practice of their true and liberating realities; by punishing, deriding, and negatively reinforcing the reclamation and manifest behavioral expression by Afrikan persons, groups, and organizations. In addition the White supremacist establishment, through its control of the domain of discourse of information and its general power to define reality, excludes the truth and beauty of Afrikan history and culture from its own and the collective consciousness of Afrikan peoples. It thereby effectively denies their existence or the worthiness of Afrikan history and culture. Their contribution to the collective character of Afrikan peoples is thereby negated and repressed, consequently distorting their cultural soul and cultural essence.

Moreover, dominant White regimes have (and do) so expertly and consistently associated the history and culture of Afrikans with the evocation of feelings of shame, guilt, anxiety, betrayal, alienation, fear of social disapproval, mental and physical abuse, social ridicule, loss of social and economic status, humiliation, and all other types of aversive emotions and consequences, until in pursuit of ego- and self-defense many Afrikans have (and do) feel compelled to reject and repress the search for the discovery of a true liberating knowledge of themselves — thus creating the social amnesia which makes them behave like reactionary puppets strung along by the machinations of their dominant White puppeteers. This "compelled" social amnesia on the part of subordinate Afrikans (which is facilitated by parental and subcultural modeling and conditioning throughout the life-span) not only disallows the discovery and reclamation of true self-knowledge by Afrikans themselves: It also disallows the discovery and exposure of the true, infamous history and culture of White supremacy and of those pathologically depraved Whites who are its perpetrators. Ultimately, the repression of a true knowledge of self, i.e., of Afrikan history and culture in subordinate Blacks, is tantamount to the repression of a true knowledge of reality — the one true foundation upon which psychological and social sanity must be constructed.

The historical/cultural amnesia imposed on the collective Afrikan psyche by the repressive White supremacist regime results not only in the sheer forgetting of their past but also in their failure to learn from it; their failure to utilize it in their reckonings regarding reality and their appropriate relationship to it. The imposed social amnesia of Afrikans markedly reduces their capacity to know the murky side of the history and culture of their White oppressors. It leaves them without an historical/cultural basis for engaging in realistic and beneficial assessments of themselves and of others, for establishing corroborative expectations regarding their own behavior and that of their Caucasian nemesis. Furthermore, the compelled social amnesia results in the absence of self-knowledge as well as in the impairment of a related sense of purposive and meaningful existence. The absence of a functional knowledge of their cultural/historical past not only blinds Afrikans to important aspects of past realities but also to crucial, critical aspects of contemporary and future realities. Thus, they are easily beguiled and misdirected by their oppressors and their own ignorance to the benefit of their exploiters — and consequently to their own detriment.

In being forced to lose their past Afrikans are, in effect, forced to lose the priceless wisdom and invaluable coping skills so painstakingly accumulated over aeons of trial and error by their ancestors. They are thus forced to "re-invent the wheel" invented centuries earlier by their forbearers. Social amnesia destroys the sense of continuity, the foundation of personal and collective identity. Consequently, the consciousness of the Afrikan amnesiac is marked by discontinuity and disconnections, episodic experiences and views of reality — the most important of which are unsystematically clustered together, unorganized by axiomatic principles and concepts.

Afrikan social amnesia impairs long-term, conceptual, sequential, relational, cause-and-effect, abstracted thinking, since this style of thinking is developed through the practiced, systematic, detailed consideration of reality of the near and distant past and its relationship to present and future reality. Consequently, perhaps too much of subordinated Afrikan thinking is relatively limited to the present, the immediate, the short-term, and marked by insufficient insight as well as foresight. It is a distracted, absent-minded, forgetful consciousness. And these characteristics enhance its readiness to identify with a falsified image of history, culture, and self concocted by the characterizations of its White creators — creators who exploit its fabricated identities and confusions for their own material benefits and self-aggrandizement. The lability and malleability of the subordinated Afrikan amnesiac permits his consciousness and behavior to be rather easily and quickly molded, shaped and impelled to obsessively pursue the latest commercial fads and fashions and social behavioral styles in further pursuit of an ever-receding, ever-changing, illusory identity — to the economic and social benefit of his White exploiters.

Finally, the reinforced social amnesia of the subordinated Afrikan permits him to absent-mindedly, obsessively seek to assimilate; to eat with, sleep with, live among, "be just like"; to identify with the captors, torturers, enslavers, lynchers and race-baiting sadistic exploiters of his ancestors and of himself as his highest achievements in life, as the eschatological finality of his being. In his "sweet" forgetfulness he is no longer motivated to seek revenge, reparation, restitution, or reconstruction for past and present wrongs perpetrated by his White oppressors; he is not motivated to construct a new, Afrikan-centered, humane utopia on the shattered remains of White supremacy's evil empire but to become an equal partner in it to become one with it — thus sanctioning the annihilation of the personhood of both his ancestors and himself. The pursuit of this "impossible dream" by the Afrikan amnesiac supplies the motive force which advances and enriches White supremacy and therefore perpetuates his own subordination and impoverishment. Thus the subordinated Afrikan does not indict the supremacist regime for its misdeeds and require it to atone for its sins. Its constituents are left blameless and guiltless — having committed the *perfect crime* against Black humanity. These are but some of the benefits to White supremacy afforded by Afrikan amnesia.

Delusion   false beliefs held by an individual which are stubbornly retained and defended despite their logical inconsistencies with objective reality and valid evidence to the contrary. Not only do such beliefs persist directly in the face of contradictory evidence, they persist in the face of continuous negative consequences resulting from their being held.

Dominant Whites have from the distant past up to the present moment unabatingly continued to propagate historical and cultural falsehoods (concerning things Afrikan as well as European) as truths, fabricated evidence to support such confabulations and lies, continued to obscure reality and conceal their inhumane motives behind a *papier-mâche* facade of humanity and hypocritical moral superiority. The creation, presentation, and sinister manipulation of powerful cultural images and ideas, information and ideology, symbols and values, rewards and punishments, social communications and interactions, have allowed Whites by dint of their overwhelming social power, to inculcate their subordinate Afrikan subjects with detrimental delusions whose attitudinal-behavioral expression advance the interests of White supremacy. Dominant Whites utilize such inculcated delusory images, ideas, values, ideologies, etc., to justify their supremacy as well as to convince themselves and their Afrikan subjects that they only have themselves (or fate perhaps?) to blame for their inferiorization. As the continuity of White supremacy is premised on the acceptance by Afrikans of the European falsification of Afrikan history and culture as true, so does its continuity also depend on their continuing acceptance of European self-serving ideological fabrications as true. In fact, in order for Afrikans to remain in their positions of subordination they must be compelled (most efficiently if achieved subliminally) to *mis*take certain Eurocentric lies for truths and certain Afrocentric truths for lies. For it is this fundamental *mis*take which inverts and reverses the subordinated Afrikan collective personality.

The virtually unchallenged social power wielded by the White supremacist establishment enables it to block out, censor, degrade, and deny the truth and severely limit the dissemination of all important, positive information, ideas, ideologies, values, etc., relative to Afrikans, except those which are compatible with and supportive of White superiority. Furthermore, the White supremacist establishment's ability to associate a full range of socially and psychologically aversive outcomes with the belief in and expression of ideologies, which if actualized by Afrikans would revolutionize Afrikan-European power relations, is utilized to motivate Afrikans to reject the holding and expression of such beliefs as hazardous to their well-being. Conversely, their ability to make relief from suffering aversive outcomes; the receipt of future material and non-material rewards, some modicum of security, social acceptance, and the like, contingent on the belief in and expression of established, self-serving Eurocentric ideologies, is utilized to motivate Afrikans to hold fast to such beliefs as ensuring their well-being. Consequently, the measure of the truth value of an ideology, belief, value, etc., in the subordinate Afrikan mind is neither determined by the degree to which it accurately represents objective reality nor by the degree to which it may equalize or revolutionize the power relations between Whites and Blacks. The basis for belief is not truth but expediency — the measure of pain or pleasure its holding and expression may bring to its host. The basis for the acceptance or rejectance of an idea becomes its emotional consequences rather than its truth value.

Related to delusion is fantasy — the conscious and unconscious creating of images, wishes, hopes, scenarios, illusory thoughts and goals and their "acting-out" either only in the mind, or in their ritualistic, fetishistic "acting-out" in reality as substitutes for desires and hopes which cannot be gratified in actuality. Fantasy fills the vacuum of absent reality. It is a pretense, a passive or active charade, the pretentious living and acting of a daydream, a substitute for action, a hope tenaciously clung to in the face of hopelessness. An escape from stress and frustration, fantasy gratifies frustrated desires by imaginary or substitute achievements — by defending the ego against paralyzing despair. Thus the easier accomplishments of make-believe are substituted for the harder accomplishments of real-life endeavors. At that point fantasy becomes self-defeating, maladaptive, and self-destructive. Yet these fantasies become the characteristic fantasies of both the "normal" and "abnormal" oppressed.

Frustration and reaction fantasies are the hallmarks of oppression. To be oppressed is to have the most meaningful wishes, hopes, plans and expectations blocked and unfulfilled by oppression or the oppressive circumstances the oppressor erects and maintains. However, the reactionary fantasies and fanciful charades of the oppressed, their pursuit of vain hopes, addiction to substitute gratifications, energize and support the oppressive regime and help to maintain their own oppression. Their religion, handed-down by their oppressors, promises them rescue, a messiah, a Moses, "pie-in-the-sky" — and thus their revolutionary will is pacified. They wait on the Lord, the tribulation, and are gratified by religious ecstacies. Their oppressors are thus permitted to enjoy heaven-on-earth at their expense.

Religions become the opiates of the oppressed and conversely, opiates become their religions, and their addiction to both materially benefits their oppressors and exploiters. The fantasy, nursed in the overheated imagination of oppressed Afrikans and often hypocritically encouraged by their oppressors, that they and their oppressors will one day live blissfully as one, is the most pernicious hoax of all. It motivates many Afrikans to blithely nurture and protect a system which exploits and blinds them to its intrinsically evil purpose, and its ultimate deadly intent. Thus, compensatory fantasy under oppression often comes to characterize, as a necessary adjunct to the oppressive regime, the "normal" consciousness of the oppressed.

Symptoms Reflecting Emotional Disturbances

Pathological anxiety	fears and anxieties which are grossly out of proportion to the actual dangers posed to any realistic danger or threat. Fear or dread resulting from an over-estimation of threat. Anxiety or dread of such overwhelming proportions that the individual feels compelled to deny or distort the portion of reality with which he associates such feelings, or to engage in self-deceptive, escapist and avoidant behavior as means of reducing or eliminating those feelings. Anxiety such that personal growth in important areas is blocked or retarded, or that the individual feels compelled to engage in anesthetizing, self-defeating and/or other forms of self-destructive behavior.

To be oppressed is to make *how* one feels or *expects* to feel, the measure of all things. To be oppressed is to be ruled through one's feelings and emotions. It is to be exquisitely exposed to and manipulated by a play on one's dreads and fears by one's oppressors; by a play on one's needs for respite from their terror; by a play on one's needs for catharsis, solace, and compensatory joy. Anxiety is the whip in the hand of the oppressor used to drive the oppressed to completion of their appointed rounds.

The ultimate power of White domination and social control resides in their ability to successfully *intimidate* subordinated Afrikans; to convince them of the *inevitability* of White supremacy; of the awesome *invincibility* of White power. The history of White-Black social relations has been one of unrelenting intimidation, terror, mental and physical abuse of Black peoples, White-on-Black violence; of endemic injustice, and of the unending, unrequited attempts by subordinate Afrikans to avoid, escape, or some way prevent, temper or ameliorate the horrendous aftereffects of these activities. Avoidance and escape from White-instigated anxieties preoccupy the consciousness and subconsciousness of oppressed Afrikans. This preoccupation pathologizes, i.e., imbalances, the Afrikan psyche. Consequently, even the "normal" Afrikan under White domination is primarily motivated by the desire to escape — to actively or passively avoid or in some other way neutralize or alleviate the fearful effects of his oppression. By definition, White supremacy requires that Blacks be primarily motivated by anxiety and its avoidance in the interest of their White oppressors.

Under White supremacy the operative presence of anxiety in the individual and collective psyche is a necessary constant. This is the case, whether these psyches be adjudged "normal" or "abnormal." They are both pathological states, primarily defined by their different anxiety-ridden structural dynamics.

It should be noted that in the subordinated Afrikan personality whether diagnosed as "normal" or "abnormal," much of the presence and operation of pathological anxiety is unconscious, i.e., unknown to its host. The subordinated Afrikan is hardly aware that his psyche, consciousness, and behavior have been subverted and misdirected by the eurocentrically-conditioned operation of anxiety and its related psychological aftereffects (other symptoms). White supremacy works most efficiently when subordinated Afrikans feel that they have freely chosen to think and behave the way they do when in actuality they have been subliminally compelled to do so by the psychopolitical machinations of their White oppressors. Thus, the subordinated Afrikan feels free*st* when he is most controlled. And his pursuit of apparent freedom is often the pursuit of unapparent enslavement.

Anxiety is the principal chisel by means of which dominant Whites attempt, with some measurable success, to sculpt the modal personality of dominated Blacks. The consciousness of subordinated Afrikans is reactionarily bent into shape by its customary defenses against the anxiety attacks leveled at it by their European oppressors. Consequently, the personalities of many, if not most, subordinated Afrikans are little more than elaborate defense mechanisms against oppressive anxieties and stresses. These mostly unconscious defense systems against oppressive anxieties have been so organized and automatized that the "normal" subordinated Afrikan experiences relatively little overt or conscious anxiety. They then stereotypically operate in ways which inadvertently help to maintain the White supremacist regime which oppresses them — the very source of their shaping anxieties to begin with.

Anxiety negates possibilities and stunts the growth and range of the self of the oppressed. Thus the oppressed personality is defined more in terms of non-being than of being; in terms of what it is not rather than what it is; its lacks, rather than its amplitudes.

Under White supremacy the subordinated Afrikan self comes into being principally to preserve a sense of security, to protect against anxiety.

> Thus, *constriction and impoverishment of personality make it possible to avoid subjective conflict and concomitant anxiety.* But the person's freedom, originality, capacity for independent love, as well as his other possibilities for expansion and development as an autonomous personality are renounced in the same process. By accepting impoverishment of personality, one can buy temporary freedom from anxiety, to be sure. But the price for this "bargain" is the loss of those unique and most precious characteristics of the human self.
>
> ...*the positive aspects of selfhood develop* as the individual [or a people] confronts, moves through, and overcomes anxiety-creating experiences.[11]

Apathy   a *dis*ease of feeling, emotion or interest; a pathology of sensitivity, energy and initiative; an absence (*a*=without) of feeling (*pathos*=feeling); an indifference to, a wont of feeling for, interest in, or responsivity to, situations that normally would be expected to evoke the opposite reactions.

---

[11] May, Rollo. 1977. *The Meaning Of Anxiety*. New York: Simon and Shuster.

Apathy is of special concern when it involves a lack of interest in learning or doing those things which if learned or done could resolve important problems confronting the apathetic individual. Apathy is learned behavior, a form of conditioned laziness and helplessness. It is the attitudinal-behavioral product of a special form of social-emotional conditioning; a form of learned fear and anxiety.

In the context of the domination of Blacks by Whites, apathy is a necessary adjunctive product of White supremacy. That is, its operative presence in subordinated Afrikans is necessarily induced in them by their White oppressors because it helps to maintain their continuing subordination.

As we noted in our discussion of pathological anxiety, the holding and expression of certain feelings, attitudes, intentions, desires, and the pursuit of certain goals by the oppressed are consistently disapproved or are associated with aversive consequences by their oppressors when such orientations run contrary to their oppressors' perceived interests. Consequently, the well-conditioned subordinate, utilizing apathy as an ego-defensive maneuver, avoids through emotional flight or escape, emotional detachment, disinterest, or indifference — those feelings, attitudes, interests and pursuits which if fully actualized and expressed would undermine the oppressive regime. Thus, apathy becomes a protective device utilized by the subordinate to defend his vulnerable ego, self-esteem, and well-being as well as to defend the system which oppresses him.

Apathy as generated by the regimes of White supremacy is rarely all-pervasive or generalized in their "pathologically-normal" Afrikan subjects. Their characteristic apathies tend to be fairly specific to certain interests and pursuits. In fact, close observation will reveal that subordinated Afrikans are conditioned by their White oppressors to demonstrate a lack of feelings for and an interest in acquiring, learning, or doing those very things which if acquired, learned or done would lead to the revolutionary overthrow of White supremacy. Thus, apathy in subordinate Afrikans essentially involves the political-economic organization of their tastes, interests, attitudes, energies, enthusiasms and sensibilities, in ways which help to perpetuate the reign of White supremacy. However, as in the case of pathological anxiety, this type of organization and its operative outcomes as reflected in Black consciousness and behavior are in the main subliminal and unconscious, and therefore are made to appear to have originated spontaneously from the primordial Afrikan character and/or modal Afrikan culture. Thus it appears only coincidental, or that as a result of a natural lack of ability, talent, or interest that apathetic Blacks do not invest the necessary time and energy in those activities which would enable them to success-fully challenge White supremacy. To the contrary, it appears they invest inordinate amounts of time and energy pursuing those activities which ultimately enrich and empower their White oppressors. Apathy in subordinated Afrikans provides White supremacy its strongest bulwark against defeat. *The greatest struggle of oppressed Afrikans is not against their White oppressors but against their own apathy.*

Symptoms Reflecting Disturbances in Motivation and Values

Alienation   to feel estranged or separated from; indifferent or hostile toward; unfamiliar with; fearful of; with-drawn from; unconnected to; to have lost remem-brance or accurate knowledge of and identity with one's true, undistorted self, historical self and culture, and important segments of reality. Loss of sense of self. The irrational feeling that one is someone else, that one's body is grotesque. Feel-ings of aimlessness, normlessness, purposeless-ness, hopelessness, meaninglessness; of being unmotivated by one's own self-originated needs and values; of being compelled or retarded by unknown, unknowable, but irresistible forces.

To be oppressed is to be forced to exist not for oneself but for the other; to support one's enemies and oppose oneself and one's fellows. To be oppressed is to have one's worthiness and esteem measured in the currency of one's oppressors — to have one's value measured in coin and utility, exclusively. The oppressed are compelled to act not for their own reasons; not in order to realize their own god-given potentials or their own self-defined, self-determined values; but for reasons imposed on them, and to realize values defined for them by their oppressors. Oppression requires the dissociation of the oppressed from themselves; that they deny themselves, in service to their oppressors; that they avoid identifying with their original personality and perceive identification with it as detrimental to their survival. The rejection of their authentic selves on the part of the oppressed is a necessary preparatory step to their replacement by artificial, manipulable selves socially manufactured by their oppressors. Alienation of the oppressed requires that they identify with these "jack-built" selves, and strive compulsively to satisfy their artificial, self-defeating, often self-destructive, motives, desires and values. Their oppressor-motivated strivings are functionally designed to enrich and empower their oppressors while simultaneously impoverishing and enfeebling themselves. The oppressed cannibalize themselves in order to feed the insatiable appetites of their oppressors.

The exploitative domination of Afrikans by Europeans exists "as something abstracted from a social matrix, apart from the web of tasks, obligations, affections, and collective relationships, which give people their identities, their social meaning, and their experience of humanity and of themselves."[12] *An Afrikan cannot truly be an Afrikan and at the same time a domesticated slave or subordinate of the European.* Thus, his domesticated subordination is inversely related to his alienation. One cannot exist without the other. Hence, the power and the glory of White supremacy pyramidally rests on the foundations of eurocentrically induced Afrikan alienation. If White supremacy is to appear normal or natural, then alienation must appear normal or natural — the apparent normality of one depends on the apparent normality of the other.

---

[12] Parenti, M. 1978. *Power and the Powerless.* New York: St. Martin Press.

The overcoming of alienation through the discovery and reclamation of their true identity and consciousness by oppressed Afrikans, portends the clattering downfall of White supremacy. It is principally to guard against this eventuality that the White supremacist establishment feels compelled to maintain Afrikan alienation as an everyday matter of course — as the central facet of Afrikan "pathological normalcy." States of consciousness and related behavior in Afrikans which contract or extends the range of this "pathological normalcy" below or beyond Eurocentric utilitarian limits is branded "abnormal" by the mental health establishment. The imposition of this label authorizes and prescribes additional social control procedures under the guises of "treatment" and "rehabilitation" in the final interest of maintaining the White supremacist social order.

Index

Aaronson 41, 42

Abnormal 73, 102, 104, 106, 108, 112, 120, 120, 127, 129, 134

Abnormality 102, 103, 106, 120

Abuse 122, 128

Afrika 66, 83

Afrikan: centered consciousness 59, 60, 111, 112, 114, 116; consciousness 2-4, 112-114 *See also* Black consciousness; history 2, 14, 19, 23, 24, 29, 31, 35, 58, 59, 114, 122, 123, 126; philosophy 59, 60; psyche 123, 129; tradition 48, 52, 54, 59

Alienated knowledge 43

Alienation 36, 54, 55, 122, 132, 133, 134

Aliens 43, 52, 114, 115

Altered States 24

Amnesia 1, 31, 33-36, 38, 39, 40, 43, 46, 52, 121, 122, 123-125

Amsterdam News 83

Apathy 75, 85, 130-132

Authority 33, 89, 104, 105, 107, 108

Ballots 13

Bank 46, 50

Banking 46-49, 51

Bennett, L. *Black Power U.S.A.* 7, 9-12, 61

Black: bank 46; consciousness 12, 99, 101-103, 113, 120, 122, 132; gover-
nor 10; history 13, 14, 38, 43, 76, 86; mayors 12; power 7, 9, 11, 14, 61; Reconstruction 11; sheriffs 10

Body politic 116

Brain (lobotomy) 83

Brainwashing 20, 54

Business crime 78

Cameroon (business financing) 45-48, 54

Canceling the present 42

Capitalism 45, 47, 56, 61, 81

Capitalist 18, 60, 81

Career-criminal 90

Civil rights laws 10-12

Civilization 14, 58, 94

Cognitive dissonance 74

Collective: pathology 101; psychology 1

Columbus 33

Compelled social amnesia 123

Compensation 83, 84

Competence 69, 74, 105, 115

Complex 28, 31, 71, 76, 110

Concealment of history 25

Conditioning 16, 17, 122, 131

Conrad, P. (in) *Critical Psychiatry* 107

Consciousness 1-4, 10, 12, 27, 29, 33, 43, 52, 58, 59, 60, 96, 99, 101-106, 109, 114, 116-118, 120-124, 128, 129, 132, 134

Contradictions 33, 67, 73, 74, 77-80, 83-85

135

Other Books By Amos Wilson

Awakening the Natural Genius of Black Children
ISBN 1-879164-01-9
PB. Pages: 144

The Developmental Psychology of The Black Child
The best-selling text on Black child development.
ISBN 0933524-01-3
PB. Pages: 216

Blueprint For Black Power: A Moral, Political and Economic Imperative for the Twenty-First Century
Masterful, nothing less than brilliant!
ISBN 1-879164-06-X
PB. Pages: 912
ISBN 1-879164-07-8
HC. Pages: 912

Afrikan-Centered Consciousness Versus The New World Order: Garveyism in the Age of Globalism (with maps)
A splendid introductory text on the continued survival of Afrikan Nationalism in the face of the new imperialism.
ISBN 1-879164-09-4
PB. Pages: 141

Black-on-Black Violence: The Psychodynamics of Black Self-Annihilation in Service of White Domination
A piercing insight into the nature and causes of Black-on-Black violence.
ISBN 1-879164-00-0
PB. Pages: 224

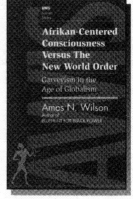

•See the following pages for order forms

CK-ON-BLACK VIOLENCE: The chodynamics of Black Self-Annihila- in Service of White Domination esents a distinct milestone in criminol- and Afrikan Studies. It theorizes that perational existence of Black-on-Black nce in the U.S.A. is psychologically economically mandated by the White rican-dominated status quo. The inalization of the Black American male psychopolitically-engineered process ed to maintain dependency and rela- powerlessness of the Afrikan American Pan-Afrikan communities. Wilson, nd blaming the victimizer, exposes the hosocial and intrapsychical dynamics ack-on-Black criminality.

PB. Pages: 224

EPRINT FOR BLACK POWER: A al, Economic and Political Impera- for the 21st Century details a master for the power revolution necessary for k survival in the 21st century. *Blue- t...* illuminates that Afrikan Americans home nearly $500 billion yearly of the ons they generate yet retain merely 5% is income. Viewed as a nation their omy would be 8th or 9th largest in the d! Wilson argues that were the Afrikan rican community to view itself as a *de* nation and organize as such, then its rges of poverty, disemployment, e, mis-education, consumerism, mis- rship and powerlessness would be ically reduced. He deconstructs and itimates the U.S. governmental and r elite structures, debunks ethno- ism, global imperial capitalism and portent for Blacks, also roundly casti- the ineptitude of Black sycophantic ous and political leadership.

ueprint warns of Black obsolescence coming millennia! It mandates and cts searing, radical approaches and rtunities for true Black Power glob- Library HB/ PB. Pages: 912

KENING THE NATURAL GENIUS LACK CHILDREN. Afrikan children aturally precocious and gifted. They life with a "natural head start." Intel- e is not fixed at birth. There is clear ace that the quality of children's

educational experiences during infancy and early childhood are substantially related to their measured intelligence, academic achievement and social behavior. Wilson reveals the daily routines, child-rearing practices, parent-child interactions, games and play materials, parent training and pre-school programs which have made demonstrably outstanding and lasting differences in the intellectual, academic and social performance of Afrikan American children.   PB. Pages: 144

THE DEVELOPMENTAL PSYCHOLOGY OF THE BLACK CHILD

- Are Black and White children the same?
- Is the Black child a White child who happens to be "painted" Black?
- Are there any significant differences in the mental and physical development of Black and White children?
- Do Black parents socialize their children to be inferior to White children?

This pioneering book looks at these and other related controversial questions from an Afrikan perspective. The topics of growth, development and education are scholarly explored.   PB. Pages: 216

New Release

AFRIKAN-CENTERED CONSCIOUSNESS VERSUS THE NEW WORLD ORDER: Garveyism in the Age of Globalism consists of two spellbinding lectures buttressed by a scintillating overview. This modest text challenges the all too pervasive assumption and false perception that the "New World Order" is somehow ordained; that if Afrikan people are to progress, they have no other alternative but to remain colonized by White Western interests. This of course is patently false. Dr. Wilson debunks this myth with an insightful analysis of the Legacy of Marcus Garvey and the proven validity of Afrikan-centered consciousness as necessary psychological and material tools in the struggle for true liberation.

Wilson puts forth his argument in ways that grab the general reader and simultaneously reduces the much-touted strategic thinking of the proponents of the New World Order to the newspeak it really is.

PB. Pages: 152

Brother
AMOS N. WILSON
1941–1995

"Disseminators of information about
Afrikan people, from Afrikan people, to Afrikan people".

Afrika
Europe
The Caribbean
North, South and
Central America
and the
Pacific Islands

Afrikan World InfoSystems was the creation of Dr. Amos Wilson with the hope that Afrikan people everywhere would become the masters of their tomorrows.

The Falsification of Afrikan Consciousness: *Eurocentric History, Psychiatry an the Politics of White Supremacy*

ISBN 1-879164-01-9	Soft Bound	Price **$13.**
ISBN 1-879164-11-6	Case Bound	Price **$23.**

• If ordering via mail please complete this order form and mail with remittance to address provided below. Note that prices are subject to change *without* notice.

Quantity & Title of Books	Unit Price		Total
	Subtotal		$ _____
	Sales Tax (NY only) 8.25 %		$ _____
	*Shipping & Handling		$ _____
	Total Order		$ _____

OTHER BOOKS BY AMOS N. WILSON

	ISBN	PR
Black-on-Black Violence	1-879164-00-0	$1
Awakening the Natural Genius of Black Children	1-879164-01-9	$1
Afrikan-centered Consciousness versus the NW Order	1-879164-09-4	$1
Understanding Black Adolescent Male Violence	1-879164-03-5	$7.
The Developmental Psychology of the Black Child	0-933524-01-3	$1

*Shipping & Handling depend on the number of books purchased — see below

1 Book $4.95	3-5 Books $8.95	6-10 Books $12.

Blueprint For Black Power	1-879164-06-X	$3
Blueprint For Black Power (Hard Cover)	1-879164-07-8	$6

*Shipping & Handling depend on the number of books purchased — see below
1 Book $5.95   2-5 Books $10.95
For case quantities please call customer services at the phone number below.

To Order by **Telephone** call **718 462-1830**
E-mail: Afrikanworld @aol.com
To Order by **Mail:**
Just fill out the information below and send this page with your remittance to:
Order Dept.
Afrikan World InfoSystems
743 Rogers Avenue, Suite 6
Brooklyn, New York 11226

Name _____

Address _____

City _____ State _____ Zip _____

Certified Check/Money Order enclosed for _____ Pay to: Afrikan World InfoS